For Kristie -

to golden Eggs!

10·5·01

THE CONFIDENCE FACTOR

COSMIC GOOSES LAY GOLDEN EGGS

mile high
press

THE CONFIDENCE FACTOR

COSMIC GOOSES LAY GOLDEN EGGS

DR. JUDITH BRILES

For ML Hanson,
One of the tallest women I know.

Books may be purchased for sales promotion
by contacting the publisher,
Mile High Press at 14160 E. Bellewood Dr., Aurora CO 80015
303-627-9179 ~ 303-627-9184 Fax ~ MileHighPress@aol.com

Library of Congress Catalog Card # 00 092831

ISBN: 1-885331-04-5

1. Success—psychology   2. Change

First Edition   Printed in the United States of America

mile high
press

Table of Contents

Prologue

Lots has happened over the past Century. Everything from medical procedures (would you like to have a heart transplant with today's methodologies or the ones used 20 years ago?), types of drugs (penicillin was introduced in the 1940s), TVs, microwaves, computers, cars, you name it; look around your home and your workplace. Little was in place prior to 1930 and in many cases, even 1960. When the new Millennium reared its head, the Internet roared.

One of the most read children's book series in the beginning of the last Century was the Oz books by L. Frank Baum. The best known being The *Wizard of Oz*. As the Century came to a close, a new challenger reared its head in the name of *Harry Potter*. Whether *Harry Potter* will be this Century's replacement, only time will tell.

In both books, there are many similarities. Harry and Dorothy are both orphaned. They both crave attention, are unhappy and both create a world of new friends. Granted Dorothy doesn't have the magical powers that Harry does but does create a little magic in her dreams. In the end, they both learn that they must take charge and be self-reliant.

Dorothy is stuck with Aunt Em and Uncle Henry, poor farmers who live in the midst of the gray Kansas prairies. There is little laughter. When Dorothy first arrives at her aunt's home, Aunt Em screams and presses her hand over her heart whenever Dorothy's merry voice reaches her ears. She cannot fathom how the little girl can find anything to laugh at in the bleak, gray environment. When the tornado swoops Dorothy and her pooch Toto up, they are transported in the old gray farmhouse to the Land of Oz—a place of brilliant color and great beauty in sharp contrast of the gloom of Kansas.

Harry is stuck with his Aunt, Uncle and bratty cousin when his parents are murdered. He is treated cruelly by the Dursleys, forced to sleep/live under a cramped stairway in their home and given minimal food. His cousin, of course, is treated like royalty, even at the dinner table. As his tenth birthday approaches, a series of letters begin to make their way to Harry. His frightened Aunt and Uncle block each one, even packing up and heading for a deserted island to escape the onslaught of letters. It doesn't work.

Finally, a message is delivered in person by Hagrid, the physical giant from Hogwarts who instructs/tells/ invites Harry to attend the exclusive wizard school. Harry had no idea he was a wizard and that his Aunt and Uncle were Muggles—non-wizards. Nor did he know that his parents had been prominent players in the world of wizards and had been murdered by the wizard's counterpart to Darth Vadar. It turns out that Harry's destiny is a key factor in the survival of Hogwarts and all future wizards.

The real life messages that I impart in *The Confidence Factor—Cosmic Gooses Lay Golden Eggs* can be drawn from the adventures of Harry and Dorothy. Their experiences have parallels to many life experiences that you will encounter.

For Dorothy, she journeyed to the City of Emeralds, found friends, developed relationships, encountered crisis after crisis, and as she traveled along the yellow brick road toward her destination, she was forced to continually reassess her situation. Her upbringing, her value system, and her life experiences became key ingredients as her own confidence was birthed and grew. Symbolically, her silver slippers (Hollywood made them ruby red) represent and remind her that she can do it . . . whatever "it" is. It's up to her.

For Harry, he lived for years in a miserable situation, hated by his Aunt, Uncle and cousin and is surprisingly uprooted and directed toward the path to Hogwarts where he encounters adventure—both the good and bad kind—time after time. At Hogwarts, he is forced to continually reassess his situation and find value in himself. His upbringing, his value system, and his life experiences became key ingredients as his own confidence was birthed and grew. Symbolically, the lightning scar on his forehead reminds him of his past . . . and his future, whatever "it" is. It's up to him.

Two different kids, two different places, two different stories, yet so much in common. Both Harry and Dorothy are brutally uprooted from the environment of their parents, alone and land in an environment that is alien to each. Today's women and men often feel uprooted, in alien territory and very alone.

When events and circumstances happen that create the upheavals in our lives, I call them *cosmic gooses*. A situation that you would most likely not want to go through again, nor would you want your friends to. Yet out of it, you are propelled and taken into another direction, a direction you most likely hadn't thought of. As you move through these new directions, situations and encounters your life is changed—personally, professionally, or both. And often, it becomes a good thing.

The Confidence Factor—Cosmic Gooses Lay Golden Eggs carries the voices of thousands of men and women. The first *The Confidence Factor—How Self-Esteem Can Change Your Life* was published in 1990. *The Confidence Factor* title was the #1 choice of my audiences to continue with—they said it tells you what the book is about! This one is all new, with new voices, a new study and new steps to create and build your confidence in the 21st Century. You will hear and read the stories that are representative of these women and men who have at times been at the depths of despair and yet climbed up to higher levels of personal and professional achievement.

Some are well known, some known well only to their circle of friends and family. Yet, you will be able to relate to them. They are real men and women. Today's men and women. Tomorrow's men and women. All have **The Confidence Factor** and all have encountered some form of a *cosmic goose* in their journey.

Chapter One

What's Your Confidence Quotient?

The year 2000 is etched in just about everyone's mind. Whether it was getting ready for it with the threats of a Y2K assault, watching the media hype the first Presidential election or even licking your wounds from the decline in your technology stock portfolio, the year 2000 will stand out. Confidence . . . your ability to confront, deal with and grow through events that you sometimes don't create or control, comes into play.

In 1990, I shepherded my first national survey on confidence. Thousands of men and women generously gave their time and allowed me to probe a variety of areas that related to confidence. Back then, when I asked, "Where does confidence come from?" men were more inclined to say "upbringing" (46%), where women were more inclined to say "experience" (43%).

The New Survey Says . . .

Today, with 1337 women and men responding to a new survey by our cut off date, "experience" jumps to the forefront with 52% of women respondents and 54% of men stating so. Upbringing now trails at #2 with 26% of women reporting so; more men than women stated that upbringing was key at 35%, a reversal of the two since the beginning of the nineties. Maturity ranked #3 with 16% for women and 9% for men and crisis at #4 with 5% of the women and 2% of the men reporting such. Genes . . . a tiny hiccup at 1% for women and 0% for men.

So, what does this mean? A turnabout, to say the least. Ten years have passed, the workplace is a different workplace; the stock market ended the decade with a roar; the Internet promises a whole new way of doing business; a new way of working emerged where the Baby Boomers had previously coined the phrase workaholic, Generation Y, the Millenniums or the Nexters (whichever term you choose) said, "Not me. I want a life."

Other Factors

In the original survey, other factors were noted. Primarily, relationships (being in one was more important to men than women); listening (having another who listens was more important to women than to men); and appearance (looking good was more important to women than to men).

The most recent survey shows no change with the relationship and listening factors. Men reported that their confidence levels were high when they were in a relationship with another. In fact, many reported that they were able to earn more money when in a relationship. Women have consistently reported that having someone to listen to their issues, concerns and dreams was an important factor in enhancing their self-esteem.

In the past, appearance ranked higher for women. Today, the appearance factor ranked high with both. Women also felt that appearance was stressed more in job interviews than men did. According to Procter & Gamble Research, July 2000, consumers believe clothing that is wrinkled says that the wearer is sloppy, unprofessional and reflects an attitude of not caring.

Appearance becomes a communicator—if you look good, you'll feed good. Golf superstar Tiger Woods would agree. He said in an interview in *Golf Digest*, September 2000, "Success thrusts you onto the world stage, and you have to be mindful of your appearance—and just as important, your image. I enjoy dressing nicely and doing my own laundry, including ironing my clothes. I still haven't quite mastered the perfect crease, though." So, I suspect Tiger doesn't go in for the wrinkled look!

Today, we are older, hopefully wiser. Since my first book on confidence was published in 1990, I have spoken to cumulative audiences of 200,000 plus women and men. Times have changed. It's a different workplace. It's a different workforce. And it's a different attitude than the previous decades.

Although men and women say that confidence comes primarily from experience, which includes the good, the bad and the ugly, their responses indicate that their confidence levels are not higher than they were ten years ago. Men are more inclined to say that there is no major difference in confidence levels of men and women (55%); women say there is (67%).

The Confidence Quiz

Where are you in the scheme of things when it comes to confidence—highly confident, scraping the barrel or in between? *The Confidence Quiz* below will take you only a few minutes to complete. Use it as an assessment to help you in understanding where you are and where you need to build yourself up.

As you read each question, write the number in the blank that best reflects how you are thinking and feeling today . . . not last week or how you speculate things may be next week. It's for *now* and will become part of your guide through the confidence maze of life.

Rarely or Never	Not Very Often	Sometimes	Frequently	Yes! Most or All of the Time
1	2	3	4	5

_____ Do you enjoy and thrive in the work you do?

_____ Are you your own best friend when you make a mistake?

_____ Do you acknowledge and take credit for your own accomplishments?

_____ Do you seek out and enjoy learning new things?

_____ Are you physically and mentally healthy?

_____ Are you comfortable with the way you look—with and without clothes on?

_____ Do you limit (or eliminate) your time spent with negative people?

_____ Do you surround yourself with people you admire?

_____ Do you have a trusted friend or colleague with whom you can let your hair down with?

_____ Do others routinely seek you out for advice and support?

_____ Do others enjoy being around you?

_____ Are you able to ask for something when you need or want it?

_____ Are you comfortable seeking assistance when you need it?

_____ When someone criticizes or rejects you, do you assess it, then move on?

_____ When you have failed at something, do you maintain your visibility and stay around others?

_____ When you run into problems, do you routinely handle them (or attempt to)?

_____ Can you laugh at yourself?

_____ Do you forgive yourself for mistakes that you make?

_____ Do you spend time with people who are positive on an ongoing basis?

_____ Are you able to say "no" to someone or something that you feel uncomfortable with or negative about?

_____ Are you self-reliant, asking, doing and getting things for yourself?

_____ Do you spend time on events, activities and people you enjoy and like?

_____ Do you routinely spend time to nourish your spiritual side?

_____ Do you routinely take time off for you to re-energize?

_____ Are you money smart, learning/knowing where to get advice for your present and future money needs and how to implement what to do?

_____ Do you feel that your life is in sync—balanced with work and play?

_____ Are you upbeat and positive—is life basically a joy for you?

_____ Do you like who you are?

_____ Do you feel that you are "on track" for you?

_____ When you feel strongly (or not so strongly) about an issue or matter, can, and do you express it?

Scoring:

The maximum score you can have is 150, which means you scored a 5 on everything, which is unlikely. One of the great secrets that highly confident women and men share is that there are times that they don't feel highly confident. In fact, there are times that they feel that confidence totally eludes them. Surprised? You shouldn't be.

140-150   **Extremely Confident**—You are a Confident Woman or Man. You've learned how to get, keep and grow your confidence. Bravo!

120-139   **Frequently Confident**—You have a great deal of confidence and can gain more with just a tad of fine-tuning. More than likely, you are a leader where you work and definitely have the key ingredients to move to the top.

90-119   **So-So Confident**—You're average, which yields you an average or so-so return in what you do. Why not stretch yourself and learn something new? Review your past accomplishments. It's time for you to get a few accolades, even if you are the only one applauding.

61-89   **Not So Confident**—Your confidence is shaky. It's time for you to step back and do some probing. Ask again, "Are you 'on track' for you?" and "Are you self-reliant, asking and getting things for yourself?" Most likely, you scored 1 or 2 when you initially answered these questions in the quiz above. It's probable that others control you, with your permission. You need to trust yourself and follow your passions, not others.

Below 61   **Rarely Confident**—Yikes . . . surgery is in order! You need to surround yourself with some pluses . . . at work and at home. If friends and family are dragging you down, tell them you need some positive support, not negative criticism. Treat yourself to something new. Read a great book; attend a stimulating lecture; see a fun movie. Make a conscious effort to reach out. Aspire higher!

On individual questions, if you scored less than 3 on any one, this doesn't mean that you should reject yourself. It's merely where you are today and what's impacted you in the past. Where you choose to go tomorrow is up to you. You orchestrate what steps you set in motion.

**Self-esteem and confidence go hand-in-hand.
Self-esteem is the regard, the appreciation,
and the caring that you have for yourself.
Confidence takes it further. Confidence is the
POWER to create that respect and appreciation
and regard you have for yourself.**

Song Sung Blue

As adults, we say that when a child is born, each has the right to feel secure and safe. And that security and safety come from housing, from shelter, from feeding, from caring, and from nurturing. But, realistically, we all know that not all children get such housing, shelter, feeding, caring, and nurturing. In fact, some of you reading this may have been among those deprived. As adults, it is quite common to want to do better for your own children than what you had yourself.

I am always amazed about the ability of some to remember events as young children, as very young children, even at the toddler stage. Most of those early years are really blanks for me. My mother had multiple pregnancies, multiple miscarriages, with three brothers surviving, and I, as the lone girl. Some people might think that as the only girl in what seemed a sea of boys, I might have been spoiled; treated as princess. Not so— the males were the preferred model.

My life until my eighth birthday is basically a blank. I have only a few memories; nine to be exact. The great earthquake in Los Angeles in the early fifties; the time my younger brother was playing with fireworks and set our garage on fire and burned it and the neighbor's avocado tree down; the time I was five and tried to get on the school bus with a popsicle and the bus driver wouldn't let me; the time we got our first television set and my brothers and I were watching *The Lone Ranger* on a very big box with a small screen–black and white, of course; the time our housekeeper, Lottie, was jumping up and down at a horse race on the TV; the time Lottie took me with her to see some of her friends and family—I had never seen so many black people at one time; the time my brothers threw me in a pool to see if I could float— I learned to swim at the age of three; the time my oldest brother threw rocks at me as I ran across a field; and the time my father held me as my head was shaved waiting for the stitches required from my brother's handiwork. That's it, not a lot of excitement in a young girl's life!

As Dorothy was surrounded by the gray bleakness of her life and Harry was stuck in the closet under the stairs, my first few years were parallel. That is, until my family moved to the beach in Southern California and I met Diane Wilkinson. Diane took me home that afternoon to meet her family—three sisters and a mom and dad. When Dorothy stepped out of the house that brought her from Kansas to a Mecca of green leaves and lushness, I stepped in a door and found what I was to later call my first heart family.

The Wilkinson tribe had four daughters, no sons. Mr. Wilkinson, who immediately became Uncle Dave, had given up long ago and bought the girls train sets. Mrs. Wilkinson became Aunt Nina. Aunt Nina taught me how to sew, what a family was, and what caring was all about. Every waking moment that I could possibly spare was spent in the Wilkinson household and, if at all possible, I tried to wangle an invitation to spend the night. I would go home to change my clothes. Otherwise, the Wilkinson household became the Land of Oz to me. The difference was that Dorothy wanted to go back home—I didn't.

For the first time, I felt secure as a child. They became my parent/family substitute. For a child, feeling secure means much more than being physically protected. Feeling secure is feeling warmth, caring, nurturing, the sense that someone is glad that you are part of their life. At the time I found my Land of Oz, the only warmth and security that I had was the thumb that I sucked until I was almost eight years of age, and my cats, who were my best friends. Their purrs put me to sleep every night. Prior to that, I felt unprotected and helpless and certainly of no value—after all, I wasn't a boy!

A Child's Needs

A child strives to feel worthy, to feel love, and until this happens, it is really quite difficult for her to pursue other dreams and goals, to grow and expand outside of childhood activities. That worthiness—or worthlessness—is from parents or parent substitutes. In my case, I ended up with substitutes. Until that time I had no inkling of who I was, what I could do, what power I had, whether I even had the right to have other friends. Certainly, no one ever came home with me. It never dawned on me to bring anyone home.

Ideally, kids need to know that they are accepted by parents and family. That's when acceptance of self blossoms. For me, that acceptance didn't start until my birth family moved and I found my first heart family.

There is a big difference between the emotional life of an adult and a child. As adults, we can make decisions about feeling good about ourselves, about feeling secure about ourselves. The child has to pull those feelings from the outside; after all, where else are they going to get the modeling? As an adult, we can measure our worth in self. For children, it is going to be a reflection. Their own value will be a reflection of the recognition they receive from those immediately around them.

Life's Little Black Books

As children leave their childhood, journeying through adolescence and finally adulthood, they carry around a variety of baggage—emotional and learned. Part of my baggage was a "mental" little black book. In that little black book, I listed a series of events and items that I promised myself I would never do to my daughters if I had any. Note that I said "daughters."

Today, I am well into my fifties. As best as I can determine, my brothers had it basically okay growing up. They were brought up under the norm of those times, they were the preferred sex, they were encouraged to take the risks, to go to school, to have careers, things that they all did. I was supposed to be a mom, I was supposed to marry, to have children, and if I was going to work, it should be something like nursing or teaching.

As I hit adolescence, my birth family moved again, separating me from the Wilkinsons. I was lost, afraid, alone, feeling that I had no friends except my two cats, that no one loved me.

The following year, I became friends with Linda Briles—she was the initial link to my second heart family. Her mother, Joyce, became my second Heart Mom—an incredible woman who cares with no strings attached. From there the lessons were completed. Everything I learned about relationships, risking and stretching and empathy were shaped with Joyce's guidance. I finally tuned in to my growing strength that I was an intelligent person—the strength that would eventually allow me to do just about anything I wanted to, if I set my mind to it.

As esteem grows in adolescence, there is far less need for protection from parents. After all, haven't we all been surrounded by teens at one time or another who feel that they know best, that they know how to change the world? The term "peer pressure" enters into this phase of development. Teens are not necessarily interested in their parents' approval and recognition. Rather, the approval of their peers is sought—that's what matters.

Finally, we come to the full adult stage of the mature person. Ideally, we feel secure and worthwhile and don't need the approval and validation of others. Unfortunately, that is not always the case. Lack of support during the early years may cause many adults to feel insecure, not worthy, and to seek constant approval and recognition from other sources.

Today, my two daughters and I laugh about my "little black book" of items that I would do if I had daughters. That mental black book that was formed over 45 years ago is still as clear today as it was then. If I hadn't found—or, perhaps, I should say, they found me-the Wilkinson family as a young girl and later Joyce Briles as an emerging teen—I cannot imagine where I would be today. The sense of security, of worthiness, of appreciation and regard for myself that they seeded allowed a lonely, unwanted little girl to blossom into a caring, supporting, and nurturing adult. I thank them from the bottom of my heart.

Throughout **The Confidence Factor—Cosmic**

Gooses Lay Golden Eggs, I will reference *Keepers*, the "ahas" that I've picked from my own and others' cosmic gooses.

The 10 Steps to Building Confidence in the following pages has been created from the input of thousands of men and women. Many of them have preceded you in your footsteps, some are following. They have willingly shared some of their potholes—*cosmic gooses*—that later turned into golden eggs.

Keeper #1
*Becoming a more confident you is in your hands . . . **not** someone else's!*

Pretty powerful stuff, and yet, fairly simple in concept—let's continue with the first step in creating confidence.

Chapter Two

Step #1

Follow Your Passion . . . Be True to You

It never occurred to me that I couldn't do it, whatever it was. I always knew that if I worked hard enough, I could.
Mary Kay Ash, Founder
Mary Kay Cosmetics

When I first started writing two decades ago, I was thrilled as a new author to get notes and letters from readers. One of them was cosmetic doyenne Mary Kay Ash. Through the years, she would send notes cheering books on. I would love to say I got them for every book I've written, but I didn't. She focused on books and themes that supported her passions for women—primarily financial responsibility, self-esteem and faith. Her passion created an empire that has in turn, carved a path for millions of women to achieve their own goals.

In our survey, we asked our respondents if they walked their talk. Did they do what they say they were going to do, or did they merely offer lip service? Were they true to themselves? In the *sometimes/rarely* category, responses were equally divided—7% of the women and men said this was tough to do. When it came to *always*, 44% of the men reported so, where 31% of the women did; *often* carried more women with 61% reporting so and 49% of the men stating such.

Chutzpah 101

The first national presidential election of the new Century generated headlines of "chutzpah" proportions. Democrat nominee Al Gore selected Senator Joe Lieberman from Connecticut as his VP running mate. Chutzpah because Lieberman was the first Jew to run on a national ticket. Chutzpah because Lieberman was quite vocal in his denouncement on the Senate floor of then President Bill Clifton's stupid behavior a la Lewinsky— it didn't matter that he was a fellow Democrat. Chutzpah because Lieberman was willing to stick his neck out and say what the great majority of all his colleagues felt—Clinton was a jerk and what he did was wrong. And chutzpah because Joe Lieberman was not a cookie cutter politician—he routinely crossed over party lines to support issues and causes he believed in.

Lieberman's response about Clinton was no surprise to friends, family and colleagues. In countless interviews, including CNN, ABC, NBC, and CBS, his remarks were broadcast over and over. It was ironic that after his nomination to the Democratic ticket during the summer of 2000, none of the Republican mouthpieces could find anything negative to say about him. Lieberman has made it his policy to do the "right thing" versus the political thing.

In the nineties, I spoke at a Republican regional conference in Indiana. At it was Senator Fred Thompson who was immersed in campaign-finance hearings. Thompson shared with those attending that during the hearings Lieberman was the ranking Democrat. He said that Lieberman also believed that "the system was corrupt" and dug his heals in when the White House attempted to put pressure on him to back off his support of Thompson's hearings. Lieberman didn't.

When the Lewinsky scandal was at its height, Republican Bill Bennett routinely made all the Sunday morning talk show rounds. He repeatedly said that a President should be "a good role model, such as George Washington . . . or Joe Lieberman." For many years, Lieberman had worked closely with Bennett against the broadcasting of shows like Jerry Springer's, most rap music lyrics and the blood and guts of popular video games. The two handed out "Silver Sewer" awards—bottom-of-the-barrel prizes for creating trashy cultural merchandise.

So, what's Joe Lieberman's passion? Most will say it's his faith. Lieberman as an Orthodox Jew and views his Sabbath as his—for his family, his faith—not business, and not politics. From sunset Friday to sunset Saturday, the Sabbath is his holy day—a day of rest. As an Orthodox Jew, he doesn't ride in cars, use the phone or any electricity on the Sabbath. He has been known to walk miles to cast a vote on a Saturday roll call in the Senate. For some, it seems a tad extreme. For Lieberman, it's part of his life.

Some wondered—if Lieberman and Gore had been elected, what would happen if there was an emergency on a Friday night or Saturday? In an interview with *Time* magazine, Lieberman said, "If you have an opportunity to help people on the Sabbath, that overrides the normal prohibitions. When I was attorney general in Connecticut, they always knew on a holy day that could call me for decisions or ask me to sign papers."

Joe Lieberman's faith is the genesis of which he is. The values that are generated from it are woven into how he functions as a person for his family, his community, the Senate . . . and himself.

Senator Joe Lieberman is passionate and true to himself. He knows when, and why he should say no to something.

> *Keeper #2*
> *If you never say "no", your "yeses"*
> *become worthless.*

Skating Your Passion

When I was a kid, I was an ace skateboarder. The skateboards of 40 plus years ago are not like the slick models in every toy store. When I was kid of eight, the closest thing to a skateboard was the dissection of a traditional pair of roller skates and nailing them to a two by four. We may not have been slick, but with some paint (stickers weren't in existence), we individualized ours just the same.

Elska Sandor and Catharine Lyons created Rookie, a New York based designer and creator of skateboards and clothing. Today they're the first and only all female skateboard company. Both noted that there was no one making sport clothing for girls.

Before Rookie, Sandor was in academia. Working on her master's in Buddhist art, she assumed that the lectern would be her earnings platform. In between her studies, she realized that she was more,

> I was in London doing my master's in Buddhist art and had always thought that I was going to be a professor. But, then I realized I could start a business and it didn't have to be conventional—I could just follow my passion.

The name of their company is derived from their entry status in the world of business—rookies. In the beginning, both wore multiple hats—PR, bookkeeper, designer, distributor, cheerleader and negotiator. When the phone started to ring and orders flowed in, their hard work paid off big time. Over 500 shops in the U.S. and several countries stock their products. Both Lyons and Sandor learned that they could be true to themselves and break out of the prescribed expectations that their traditional training would have led them to. Passion makes the difference.

Walking Your Image

Prioritizing and *focusing* would be two words that describe money maven Suze Orman. Identified as one of the most influential individuals of the last decade, her books have sold in the millions. Before she became a best-selling author and media personality, was everything coming up roses for her? Nope, she's had her potholes to come through.

Last year, I spoke in Florida for NAWBO—the National Association of Women Business Owners, a conference she was the opening session speaker. That morning, not unexpectedly, her topic was about money. When Orman speaks about money, she speaks more on the philosophy of it versus the nuts and bolts and how-tos.

For someone who has made millions, Suze Orman does not surround herself as most millionaires do. She still lives in the same house she bought over 20 years ago in Oakland, California—all 1,000 square feet of it. She doesn't spend lots of money on herself and believes that you have to give to receive. Tithing is woven into her life.

In her talk, Orman credited much of who she is to her father. He had plenty of ups and downs, failures and starting over. She learned that it's OK to fail and that good things can happen, as well as bad. She learned that the only thing that matters in life is your attitude . . . and with a positive attitude, you can start over.

One of the pluses in hearing and reading the words of Orman is that she was never born with money, nor did her family give her a bunch. Early in her career, she worked for Merrill Lynch as a stockbroker. In 1983, long before her *9 Steps to Financial Freedom* was featured on

QVC, she made good money, but it wasn't the solution to what she was looking for. Orman felt a deep void, and within it her cosmic goose was laid. As she said,

> It was a bummer to realize I had all this money, and
> I wasn't really happy. That's when spirituality came
> in. It became my quest, one that I had to go on.
> It wasn't because it was the thing to do. It was
> because there was nothing left to turn to. Money is
> 'exterior'—if you can't turn to it to make you happy,
> then what do you turn to? The answer is within . . .
> you have to turn to yourself.

Orman said that she began to confront her past, her credit card debt (yes, Suze Orman had outstanding balances on her credit cards, just like most people in the U.S.!) and what influences our culture had on our money spending habits. Let's face it, America is a materialistic country. Keeping up and one bettering the Jones is a way of life for millions. It takes courage, and passion, to say enough is enough. Orman did, can you?

An Apple a Day

For 18 years, I worked in Silicon Valley. First as a stock-broker for five years; then as a Certified Financial Planner for eight years before becoming a writer and speaker on a full time basis in 1986. As an investment advisor living in Silicon Valley before the zillions of dot coms were ever heard of, there were plenty of new kids on the block. All were highly visible—Hewlett Packard, Advanced Micro Devices, Intel, etc.—all giants today. And, there was Apple Computer.

As an upstart computer company started in the garage, Apple has experienced mercurial rises and falls in the eyes of investors and their users since the seventies. Labored with Steve Jobs and Steve Wozniak as the creative geniuses and midwives, it was a wonder to watch its birth and multiple near death experiences.

John Sculley arrived at Apple to take control and lead the company into its next generation. As the then CEO, Jobs was a novice in the management game. He welcomed Sculley, working along side for several years until he was told he was the wrong fit. The affair was over and Jobs was ousted in 1985. I suspect that Jobs felt that Sculley betrayed his trust and support. Where Wozniak chose to pull out fairly early in the game; the man from Pepsi booted out Jobs.

Jobs next created NeXT, his invisionment of where the next generation of computers was going. In so many words, it basically bombed and Jobs shut it's hardware division down in 1993 with Sculley getting the boot from Apple the same year. In 1996, Apple bought NeXT and lured Jobs back as an unpaid consultant. Within a year, he was back at the helm as the interim CEO and then permanent CEO (until the next possible upheaval).

The grapevine said that Jobs was a has been—washed up and an all too brief flash in the Silicon Valley frying pan. Little did the tongue waggers know where Jobs' genius was going to pop up next. Today, he's the power and CEO of two leading companies that are major forces in their respective industries. In 1986, he purchased a stake in a struggling company from George Lucas, reigning galaxy visionary flick guru. It's first full-length film, *Toy Story,* made box office history plus put digital-animation as a major competitor to traditional hand-drawn animation a la Disney. The company is Pixar Animation Studios and is "the one" that is likened to become the next Disney.

There isn't a single man or woman who better exemplifies the roller coaster path of Silicon Valley than Steve Jobs. He was at the top of the game in the eighties (I can remember a full page ad in the business section thanking IBM for getting into the personal computer business . . . Apple was legit!); he was buried in the business rock pile a few years later and rebounded as Superman in the nineties.

Where he goes and what happens is still in his hand of life. Because of his business style (it varies between incredibly good and supportive to abusive), he's got plenty of enemies. Many would love to see him take a dive once again. No matter . . . what Steve Jobs is and does reflects his passion for what he does and what he believes in. His original vision of Apple was to bridge the gap between the average person and the computer—the person who didn't have to be a techie, just someone who might need a computer. In 1986, he sold me—I bought five Macs for my office.

Steve Jobs is passionate and true to himself.

Time for Me

Coreen Cordova is an artist . . . not the traditional artist who creates magic on canvas, yet she paints. Prior to becoming a corporate consultant, an international jewelry designer, and the West Coast Stylist for NBC, she ran one of the top-rated makeup salons in San Francisco.

During her career, she's done her mastery on the famous and not so famous. One celebrity story she shared was about the talented actress and singer Dinah Shore. Cordova says,

> Dinah Shore was lovely to everyone around her; calm, easygoing, caring. I thought, 'This is wonderful.' I asked her what kind of beauty regimen she did. Her response was that every morning she spent about two hours on herself. I was shocked that anybody would spend two hours.
>
> She said, 'I wake up and I go and exercise. It's important to keep in shape. Then I have a small breakfast and supplement it with vitamins. While eating, I read something spiritually inspiring that I can keep in my thoughts throughout the day. I then take my shower, wash my hair, apply makeup, and style my hair. I put out my wardrobe for the day, get dressed, and I'm done. This entire process takes two hours, and the reason I take two hours for myself every morning is so that I can then spend the rest of the day on everybody else!
>
> I believe that charity begins at home when it comes to loving yourself. You can't expect someone else to love you or take care of you. You need to devote a certain amount of time every day to yourself, your body, your beauty, your mind, and your spirit. Once you've gotten that, once that belongs to you, once that is part of your life, you'll feel better about giving because nobody can take away what you have given yourself.

Cordova feels that way about what she does for everyone. She makes women feel beautiful and look beautiful. Thousands of women. Now she follows Dinah Shore's advice. She takes care of her own beauty and her own body needs first. Then she is able to go out and help other women develop their own beauty. It's her passion.

The First Step

As the *10 Steps to Building Confidence* were being put together, it was clear that Step #1—Following Your Passion and Being True to You would be first. It was on everybody's list. Not just a consensus, but also a unanimous selection.

Being true to yourself requires a closer, caring, thoughtful, and probing conversation with you. Self-talk is put into play. You are the judge, the jury, and the critic. This is the time to listen quietly to your inner voice. The voice that often roars, if you allow it to.

Fear for All

Most of us have some form of fear in us. A fear that can enable others to influence, intimidate, and manipulate you into being/doing something that just doesn't fit who and what you are about. Confronting that fear is a necessary step in looking in the mirror, recognizing, knowing and accepting who you are, warts and all.

We also participate in self-fulfilled prophecies. It's not uncommon for a therapist to report that the unhappy and depressed people they see are not deficient individuals. Rather, they have a great amount of potential and depth about them. But instead of being creative and able to work, they behave as though they are not good, quasi-retarded, and even unattractive. If you are afraid of an upcoming test, or even a job interview, you can psyche yourself out and belief the worst of the worst. In the end, you fail; you guaranteed your failure—one of those self-fulfilling prophecies of life.

You may wonder—why someone would want to hide good qualities and reinforce some of the negatives? The answer is fairly simple. Once qualities are recognized, they then need to be acknowledged—they need to be used. If no one knows about those hidden qualities, no one will expect anything from you. Some feel safe in mediocrity. Another form of a self-fulfilled prophecy.

There is no perfect fixer upper or guru who can create the perfect world with the wave of a magic wand or advice. When you are honest with yourself, follow your passions, you know very well on whom you can and cannot depend. Be the grownup, not the child. Lead the parade with your banner flying—even if you think there is nobody behind you.

Keeper #3
Ask yourself—what is your joy,
your spirituality, your passion?
Only you really know. Until you ask the
question, and listen to the answer, you will
not be able to be true to yourself. Ever.

Who's leading your parade? Are you? Or is someone else? Remember that you are the author of the rest of your life. And you will attract to yourself those and that which you believe about yourself. When you ask or expect others to create your own values, you won't find who you are. Joe Lieberman didn't. Suze Orman didn't. Dinah Shore didn't. Steve Jobs didn't. Dig down. Be yourself. Be true. Be passionate. Follow your bliss. Your bliss will follow you.

Chapter Three

Step #2

Delete Negativity . . . Being Positive Isn't a Myth

I felt that this was the race, the moment. That night, when ABC rolled up all smiles under the cover of their umbrellas for an interview in the rain, I knew it was official. Nothing would hold me back. I felt so confident!

Elaine Mariolle, winner Race Across America

The obvious opposite of positive is negative. With whatever you are doing at the present time, it is critical for you to take a close look at those with whom you surround yourself, your activities, your work, your play—wherever you go.

Are the people that you are around generators of positive energy, of positive thinking? If not, they could be a major factor in you experiencing low confidence.

Negative thinking—negative energy, is like a sponge. It absorbs and consumes just about anything around it. You. These are the people that I call the energy suckers of life. They are parasites.

In The Confidence Factor Survey, we asked the question, "When you are around negative people, what do you do?" The majority of our respondents said that they *try to avoid* them (60% women and 42% men). Men were more inclined to *try to change* the negative person (42% versus women at 26%), which was a surprising result. In the past, women have put more energy into trying to change or fix another. Men were also were more inclined than woman (12% to 7%) *to do nothing* about or around negative people. The fewest responses came from the option of telling the negative person *to shape up* (7% women and 4% men).

Keeper #4
You don't need energy suckers in your life.
Accent the positive; eliminate the negative.
That includes people, places and things.

Be forewarned that misery loves company. Most of us don't like to be miserable. You want to be empathetic and sympathetic to people who are having problems. But, at some point, you're going to have to say that enough is enough. You must move on. At the same time, you have to take control. Even in the worst of times.

Getting It in Perspective

One of the biggest challenges is to put things in perspective—understand the whole scheme of life and really determine how important issues and things are, and what is bothering you, if anything. Once you start putting things in perspective, you realize that even if you lost your job, you're a healthy person. That whatever it is, the loss or pain that you're feeling actually lessens in its importance. That enables you to create a good attitude. If you don't, then the negative feelings that you're experiencing tend to create and feed additional negative feelings.

With self-talk, it's important to tell yourself that you're a loving, caring, nurturing, supporting person who believes that you yourself are great. This is a time that you concentrate on eliminating those old tapes, those little voices of your parents, your grandparents, their parents and everybody else's who would tell you that you need to do more. It's essential to have pals and cronies who are out there for you, who encourage and support you. That allows spill over. Positive creates more positive.

Total Vision

Of the 10,000 plus men and women that I have surveyed and interviewed since the late eighties, no one impressed me as Sharon Komlos did. Today, she is an author and a speaker. She will tell you she has it all. She has three kids, all adults. She has a career that she is dedicated to, makes more than enough money to support herself, and has been passionately in love with

Ray, the man in her life, for 20 years. She exudes so much confidence and trust that strangers often approach her in airports when she is waiting for her luggage, asking if she will watch theirs as they hail a cab. Komlos says she is always glad to, and then wonders what happens if it disappears. You may wonder, "Big deal, what's so special about Sharon Komlos?" Plenty.

The BIG Deal Is—She Is Blind

Twenty plus years ago, she moved from Ohio to Florida. Driving home one evening, she noted a car driving up beside her. Then, a flash of light. All of a sudden, in a nano-second, her vision was gone.

> I felt a sensation of blood dripping down my face and I couldn't see. I pulled the car over to the side of the road and I lay on the horn, hoping that a Good Samaritan would come. Within minutes, help was at the door. A man lifted me off the car horn and offered to take me to the hospital. He placed me on the rear seat floor of his car telling me that he didn't know the area well.
>
> I knew the area fairly well and I tried to direct him to the hospital. When he finally stopped, he lifted me out of the car and helped me up some stairs. Later, I realized it was his apartment. He closed the door and pushed me down on the mattress. We struggled, he tried to suffocate me. When I managed to break loose, he stabbed me in the chest, slicing my neck. Finally, he raped me. I was kept in his apartment for eight hours. When morning came, he left me for dead. I had lost so much blood that when he

checked my pulse, he must have been satisfied that my time left was very limited.

My clothes were taken. I got up, walked around the apartment, and found a way out. I started screaming. This time, a real Good Samaritan came to my rescue, and took me to the hospital. I gave a description of the apartment to the police, who made out a search warrant. The police later said he'd probably left to find a way to dispose of my body. I didn't know until later that this was the same guy who had shot me.

Before the "incident," as she refers to it, Komlos was an insurance adjuster. She did all her own investigations, even negotiations. She dealt with attorneys and went to body shops to estimate damage to cars.

When my husband called my employer the next day and told them I wouldn't be in for a few days, I was automatically let go. My desk was cleaned out before I left the hospital. I wasn't given the opportunity to prove that I was capable of continuing to do what I had done very well.

My family were victims of the crime. When the doctor told me that I would be blind for the rest of my life, I already knew. I had come to grips with the fact in the hospital. Both retinas had been destroyed.

Komlos eventually wrote a book, *Feel the Laughter,* and speaks nationwide. She was a subject of a *20/20* segment that had originally been scheduled to focus on

violence. When the *20/20* team came to hear her speak
at a school, they redirected the thrust of the program to
concentrate on overcoming adversity.

Sharon Komlos says that today she is no different
from the person that she was prior to 1980. Prior to her
"incident"!

> I'm not any different, my outlook hasn't changed,
> but my family did experience the outcome.
> Eventually my marriage fell apart—my husband had
> an extremely difficult time in dealing with what hap-
> pened. We put a lot of energy into trying to work it
> out, but it just didn't work.
>
> During my recovery, much of society expected me
> to stay down and out. Some of the professional pro-
> grams even tried to demean me. People would accuse
> me of not acting normal. My response was, 'What's
> normal?'

Komlos can tell time, uses a calculator and computer—all come in "talking" versions. She does, though,
have her limits—she says she'll never purchase a talking scale. She is not the stereotype of the blind person.
She doesn't wear dark glasses, use a cane, or have a
Seeing Eye dog. She does, though, have vision. To her,
sight is not a condition for happiness. Many people that
she's encountered have full sight. They are also blind.

To Sharon Komlos, faith and her belief in God are an
integral part of what her substance is. She focuses on
the positive and feels people need to stop victimizing
themselves. She has three basic philosophies.

First, I accept what was handed down to me. I look at it as a challenge, as something that was given to me to learn about life.

Second, I can't control the external forces around me. I can, though, control the path that my life is going to take. I have options.

And, third, there is a reason for everything. Sometimes those reasons are hidden and not apparent, especially at the time a tragedy, an accident, a situation occurs. Eventually, they will surface.

I have become an expert at overcoming. In building a new career for myself, I knew the odds were not in my favor, but I refuse to be a victim. When I am interviewed, or during the question-and-answer sessions after my speeches, many ask me how I cope. I always respond, "I don't cope. In fact, I don't like the word 'coping.' It implies that everything is at an even keel. That I merely take things as they come. The words I choose to use are 'succeeding' and 'achieving.' I go beyond coping, I achieve.

The Star of the East

Yue-Sai Kan is the most famous woman on earth. You may not have heard of her, but hundreds of millions have-for she commands the largest viewing audience in television history. Yue-Sai Kan is a Chinese-American. She is also the host-producer of *One World,* a show that 400 million people in the People's Republic of China view weekly. Another show, *Looking East,* on the Discovery channel in the United States, gives viewers an armchair view of Asia. She is so influential in China that her show is broadcast in Mandarin and English and every word printed in both languages in the Chinese equivalent of the *TV Guide.* The Chinese study her scripts like textbooks.

How did this woman become the Barbara Walters of the East? Getting there was not a bed of roses. One thing she credits is the fact that she had wonderful parents who instilled in her a sense of confidence. She was the firstborn in the family and she was allowed to stretch, test herself. She also is a firm believer in positive energy and a positive environment. She has little use for those who rain on her parade and try to circumvent her vision.

If I had listened to every negative response to my proposals I'd never have gotten to where I am today. I don't like negative people around me because I find them very depressing and destructive. Like everyone else, of course, I have had unpleasant experiences, but I don't allow unhappy thoughts to stick to my psyche. I believe in having positive images. I work hard to create them through visualization. A simple example: say, I want to interview someone very difficult to get to. I actually would go around day in and day out visualizing that I am already talking to that person. You must believe that it has always worked for me. It is positive energy that makes things happen.

When unfortunate things happen, I take a deep breath and say, 'Okay, this has happened, but this will pass. I am going to replace it with something positive.' Then I work hard at diverting myself to positive things. The faster you can move on to things that occupy your efforts (leaving no time to wallow in misery), the faster you'll get back to normality. Whatever normality is to you.

I am also a strong believer in perseverance. We approach sponsors constantly for projects that we truly believe in and sometimes we get turned down. Naturally, we get discouraged, but I only allow this unhappy feeling to last for a very short time. I have learned to immediately think and scout out other possibilities and I spend all my energy thinking about future potentials. If I keep dwelling on only the rejections, I would become scared, and it will be impossible for me to move on to try someone else. Learn to discard bad feelings immediately.

The most confident and successful people are turned down, rejected, sometimes even ignored. Those turndowns and rejections are a form of a cosmic goose. If you had your druthers, most likely you would want things to go your way—who wouldn't?

Persistence Lays the Golden Egg

Realistically, it doesn't happen all the time. A common trait found in confident and successful people is persistence. They are able to keep their confidence, or regain it when they have gone through a negative experience by persevering.

Justice Sandra Day O'Connor, Steve Forbes, Norman Lear, and Senators Dianne Feinstein and Olympia Snowe and all said that they were persistent and would keep trying when turned down. Whoever they had proposed their ideas to and were rejected by was merely not the right match. They believed that the match would occur sometime within a few days, if they were persistent in their quest. So did Elaine Mariolle.

Mariolle, victor of 1986's Race Across America, was stung when ABC's Diana Nyad interviewed her just a few days into the 1985 race.

I remember Diana Nyad approached me when I was in the eastern part of New Mexico. She said something like, 'Elaine, you made it across the country once and it looks like you're kind of out of the competition now. Is there any reason why you're continuing to go on?'

In a pre-race interview, I had told Diana that I expected to be competitive. After three days, it was clear that I had fallen short of my expectations. Diana's question identified my situation exactly. And that derailed me a bit. My reply was something like, 'I am just going to do my personal best.' In my heart, I was really disappointed and I began to think that I just wasn't good enough. I hung in there and did do my personal best, shortening my time from the previous year by three days.

Just saying the words 'I quit' scared me so much that I found myself back on the bike and pedaling east. I resolved to start over and try to make the second half of the 1985 RAAM better than the first. I wanted to make it to Atlantic City. If the crew would just give me one last chance, I would never quit on them again. It's hard to accept yourself when you are not doing a great job. It's hard to handle the fact that you're not fast enough, that you're not holding up well physically, that you aren't always nice. In the short run, quitting is easy because you don't have to deal with the realities. In the long run, though, I think there would always be the question, 'I wonder if we could have made it?'

Mariolle said that there were times when she felt as though a solid wall was in front of her during her race the previous year—her first time out. The different weather that greeted her in sections of the United States was awesome and spectacular at best, forbidding and demoralizing at worst.

> There were times during the race that I expected Dorothy, Toto, and the Wicked Witch of the West to fly past at any time. The winds and crosswinds through Kansas were spectacular. My crew sometimes had to feed me my meals bite by bite. I was afraid to let go of the bars to eat. They finally forced me to stop as I continually tried to ride against a wall of wind. I used gears in Kansas that were unnecessary climbing Loveland Pass in Colorado.
>
> Crawling into a stiff head wind hour after hour was heartbreaking. It ate at my spirit, especially when we heard reports that the lead men who passed through days before the head of the storm had enjoyed a tail wind. It was a thoroughly miserable and discouraging time.
>
> I would drop in bed with all my rain gear and

helmet on. I was out cold for a few hours, I was emotionally drained. I wanted to quit. Then, I would rationalize—we had come too far to turn back.

Despite my best intentions, I continued to flounder through Kansas. When we crossed the state line, my crew played the song *Surrender Dorothy* and *Escape from Kansas.* I was relieved to leave the flatlands and get into the rolling hills of Missouri.

At one point, I was riding on a frontage road paralleling the highway. A woman pulled off the highway and got out of the car, rushed over the chain link fence, and shouted, 'Hang in there, honey,' as I rolled by. This woman, like so many other upbeat people along the way, really gave me a boost.

After I was on the road for a few miles, the ABC crew rolled by. They all told me how great I looked. I almost died when Diana Nyad asked me if I was proud of myself even if I was in the last place. I told her, 'If last place is the best I can do this year, then that's fine.'

I knew even as I was answering her question that I could do better in the future. This would be the last time that I saw ABC. I was so far back that they had to wait half a day for me.

Perseverance. Positive thinking. Key traits for all successful, confident individuals. Mariolle's goal wasn't to win the first time she entered the Race Across America in 1984—she was testing the grounds, the course; nor did she win in 1985, although she did better her time by three days. As the 1986 race approached, she knew that this time would be different. The experience of the two previous trips would pay off.

Third Time's a Charm

She wasn't intimidated any longer by the other women contenders who had finished ahead of her. Her team was better prepared. Her entire family had joined her, including her mother and father as part of the crew. Elaine Mariolle had surrounded herself with positive support. For the first time, she believed that she was a real contender in the race.

As the race began to unfold, I was surprised by how much I had remembered. It helped experiencing the same terrain from the previous years. As I rode into the night of the second day, the ABC crew appeared out of the darkness to talk to me. They were all piled into a large van and looked a bit crowded and tired, but as usual they were upbeat.

For the third time, Diana Nyad asked me what my strategy would be. Would I plan to go without sleep and try to build a lead? My response was that I would stick to my original plan and ride to the next time station and then take a two-hour sleep break.

I was careful not to get too excited too soon. There was still a long way to go. After my sleep break, I found out that I was only eight minutes behind the leader and I was READY. When I caught up with Shelby, I was tense and excited. I had great respect for her athletic prowess and I had anticipated this moment for years. I felt that this was THE race,

THE moment. I half expected fireworks. There weren't any.

We rode neck to neck for the next two hundred miles, leapfrogging our way across the New Mexico plateau. As I pulled away into the head wind on the east side of the Continental Divide, I never guessed it would be for good. I thought she would rally back, she always had. But I felt confident. I had passed her once, and I knew I could do it again. My batteries were charged; I was turned on. That night, when ABC rolled up all smiles under the cover of umbrellas for an interview in the rain, I knew it was official. I was officially in the lead and nothing would hold me back.

Elaine Mariolle got rid of the old thoughts about herself that she couldn't make it, that she should quit, that she wasn't a winner. In 1986, she won the Race Across America—all three thousand-plus miles of it, setting a new women's transcontinental record. Ironically, her time was so good that the she was also included as an official man!

What happened from her first venture in 1984 to the winning time in 1986? Training and attitude. She changed both. In the 1984 race, she was so far behind her field that the finish line had been dismantled, the signs of welcome trashed and all had gone home. It was up to Mariolle to make the difference. She did.

In her third attempt, she was able to step aside from negative self-talk. She didn't tell herself, "I can't do this. I messed up before." She took those experiences where she had messed up in her previous races and she made them positive to prove that she was the champion she was. And is. During the race, she totally diverted all thoughts and energy away from things that she had no control over. Mariolle learned that it doesn't pay to waste your energy worrying.

She visualized herself the victor in the race. In her words, "If you visualize failure, guaranteed, that's what you get. On the other hand, if you hold the image of yourself doing something positive, as a winner, a victor, then that's what you're going to be."

Negative Energy Is the Pits— So Are Negative People

I am continuingly amazed at the number of people who embrace negative factions—whether it's their work, their relationships, the free time. Any type of negative energy is so unpleasant. You can't sleep, you worry, and it's a downer to yourself and everyone around you. Plus, it takes far more energy to be negative than it does to be positive.

Jean Kelley is a columnist, author (*Ask Jean!*) and CEO of a successful temporary placement agency in Oklahoma. She went so far as to say that you have to be careful in airports. Her experience is that one of the reasons people are so tired from traveling isn't the great stress of traveling. Rather, a lot of the people there create a negative energy field. In her words,

> Negative people are a vexation to your spirit. You can feel it. You can feel it in airports. Although I spend a lot of time traveling, I really mentally work on myself to block out the negative field that often sur-

rounds travelers. I even feel a difference when I sit in first-class versus coach. It is not always because of a more comfortable chair, a little more legroom. The people I aspire to be like are far more likely to be sitting up front versus crowded like cattle in the back.

It is also important to stay away from negative people in your family unless they are people you admire. Negative people can be like adding salt to an already open wound.

The Law of Displacement

One of my speaking cronies is Texas based management consultant and trainer Joe Charbonneau, whose expertise is in the law of displacement. Charbonneau feels that understanding the law of displacement and how it can work to your advantage is one of the keys to confidence. Negative people are the pits for Charbonneau— he's a strong believer in removing them from your life.

The mind can only occupy one thought at a time. What you choose to have in your mind will determine how you feel. In order to change the thought that occupies your mind, you must bombard it with other thoughts. That's the law of displacement—the act of replacing one thought that generates bad feelings and bombard it with thoughts that create good feelings.

If you let people rain on your parade, it will totally wipe out whatever dream machine you have. You can't stretch and grow. When I'm working with individuals, one of the questions that I bring up to myself is to ask, 'Is this person a supporter or a deserter?' My view of most people is either they are wind in my sail or they anchor my tail. People who are successful have found the habit of doing things that people who fail dislike and will not do.

Shifting Your Motion

If you look forward, you will exude self-confidence. If you think that you are in control even when you don't feel you're in control, you're able to create positive energy. When you think forward as to how you're going to do it, how you're going to handle a situation, you're able to think positively, creating positive energy that in turn helps channel whatever stress you're feeling.

When I am writing, I have standard uniforms I slip into. I like grubbies, sweat socks, or bare feet depending on the weather, loose slacks or sweats and one of those huge oversized shirts. I also like to surround myself with water. I have written books on ships. I have written chapters of books on a barge slowly moving down the canals of Holland. I have put the finishing touches on books on the shores of Maui, Lake Tahoe and Puerto Rico, and in different parts of Europe. It's what works for me, it kick-starts me with a positive attitude.

In summing up, positive thinking can be expressed in a few sentences. *Your thoughts become your words; your words become your actions.* Everyone who reads this book will experience dark moments—major potholes in their lives. There will be times of negativism in which worth is questioned, values questioned, existence questioned. When those times prevail, a positive attitude is a key factor in resurfacing, in re-breathing and reliving. The darkness the caterpillar calls the end of the world is the sun-filled moment that the butterfly will emerge. No one is born with rejection or negative on their forehead or tush, both brands get there by negative self-talk, negative environments and negative people, including self.

Keeper #5

Being positive is an attitude. There are no magic formulas or shortcuts. It's a type of self-development program. Being positive needs to start with the determination and willingness to make the effort, then allowing that effort to feed on it.

Positive people, thoughts, things and places over negative people, thoughts, things and places; or negative people, thoughts, things and places over positive people, thoughts, things and places. Which would you choose to surround yourself with? There should only be one answer.

Chapter Four

Step #3

Break the Rules . . . Be Different!

My confidence comes from age and experience. It is natural as a young person to lack self-confidence, but as we grow older, we realize that we may not care so much about how others view us and that we should be willing to trust our own judgment day-to-day. Experience in performing our jobs clearly increases our confidence level.

Sandra Day O'Connor,
Justice of the Supreme Court of the United States.

Years ago, one of my friends published *If It Ain't Broke, Break It!* Author Bob Kriegel enthusiastically told corporate America to get off their collective duffs and banish the sacred cows from their organizations. He's right. It's high time that the belly-aching is axed—change is here to stay and will only accelerate. The sooner the same old, same old is hacked at, the better for all of us.

Kriegel was an exponent of breaking the rules; doing things differently, even if things seem to be going smoothly. Smoothness with no waves of change in the foreseeable future of the organization easily leads to apathy and complacency from within. Numbness hits the workplace; few realize the necessity to spice things up a tad, to initiate change, which usually involves breaking someone's rules.

We asked our survey respondents what happens when others say they couldn't or shouldn't do something. More women said that they simply *ignored* them with 35% reporting so and 28% of the men stating the same. The majority said that they would try to *explain what and why* they were doing it with 70% of the men saying so and 62% of the women. When it came to the intimidation factor, 3% of the women and 2% of the men said that they just *wouldn't* do it.

The Billion Dollar Tiger

In the nineties, a student attending Stanford University changed the sport of golf, both for players and viewers. When Tiger Woods elected to not return to Stanford for his final year and turn pro, the world of golf initially smirked at the Kid . . . until he won the U.S. Masters a few months later—literally running away from the field of seasoned pros.

Tiger Woods was different. Yes, he was young, all 20 years of him. Yes, he was racially mixed. Yes, he has played golf since he was a toddler. That's enough to make him different, a little rule breaking, but nothing major. There have always been child protégés and talented sportsman and women of color. What was different about Woods was his discipline. He broke the rules when he came to practice and to his behavior pre-, during, and post competitions.

Woods worked out—mentally and physically. Most pros had never thought of engaging a personal trainer and faithfully working out pre, during and post their competitions. Woods stayed away from booze and practiced for several hours after a round during competitions. Typically, his fellow players would hit the 19th hole and at the end of the day and stop. Since Woods turned pro, he's influenced the physical training of golfers worldwide, all by breaking the old rules.

In 2000, Tiger Woods signed a $100 million deal with Nike, up from the $40 million deal signed in 1996. As the world's number one golfer, it's predicted that he will become sport's first billion-dollar man. He's broken all the rules, and created new ones.

The Outsider is In

Ever since I first heard the words Hewlett Packard in 1972, I learned to affiliate the company with the term "reorganization." The hundreds of clients that I worked with that were employed by H-P consistently told me that H-P was once again going through reorganization. When H-P brought in a new CEO in the late nineties, I expected that once again, reorganization would be at the top of the list.

This CEO was different than previous CEOs. This CEO didn't wear the typical suit. This CEO was a she. And this CEO had never worked in the computer industry. Carly Fiorina was the first outsider to take the reins in H-P's history.

In an interview with *FORTUNE* magazine in October of 1999, she revealed what she told the Board of Directors,

> Look, lack of computer expertise is not Hewlett-Packard's problem. There are loads of people here who can provide that. I've demonstrated an ability to pick up quickly on the essence of what's important. I know what I don't know. And I know that our strengths are complementary. You have deep engineering prowess. I bring strategic vision, which is what H-P needs.

After taking the helm, she revealed her plans for her corporate reorganization. The senior executives told her that it would take at least a year. She said it wouldn't and it can't take that long. Instead, they would have to complete it within three months. They did.

Hewlett Packard and the "H-P Way" have been ingrained in Silicon Valley for decades. The H-P Way was a revered corporate tradition that included employee support and innovation. When the company was founded in a garage by William Hewlett and David Packard, it had few epithets—employees would be treated with respect, the company would plan for the long term, not just short-term profits, and it would divvy up expanding business units when they got too large. It was well known within the Valley that H-P took care of its employees.

Managers grumbled that Fiorina didn't understand

the H-P Way. She actually did . . . she worked as a secretary at one time for the behemoth. That was before she went to taste law school (the wrong fit), went on to get her MBA and rose to the executive ranks at Lucent Technologies.

With the outsider, the H-P Way was sometimes overlooked. The outsider had different views about what the modern H-P Way should be. Within three months of her arrival, she shredded the company's profit-sharing program. The new one was based on performance versus being a given . . . if you worked there, you participated on an equal, pro-rata basis. No more, it became a performance based bonus system.

When Fiorina stepped in, there were over 80 businesses underneath the H-P umbrella. Her plan was to consolidate like businesses to 12. She also realigned the number of divisions. This wasn't the H-P Way—old-time executives, and employees went into a state of shock. Many said that the employees just weren't able to process, nor were they ready, for this degree of change.

Was there resentment?—You bet. Complaints were common around the water cooler. "She doesn't understand the business or Our Way." Many thought she would fall on her face, and do it in a brief period of time. Many hoped she would. CEOs are suppose to be leaders and lead their company to the next generation, many times not being clear as to exactly what it is and where they are going. Carly Fiorina's arrival at Hewlett Packard has made a difference. The company's growth has increased; the stock is no longer viewed as an "old lady" but as a crone with a heart transplant. Now, if earnings increase, she hits a home run.

> *Keeper #6*
> *When doing the same old, same old,*
> *you end up inhaling your own exhaust.*
> *With it, you risk stifling, paralyzing or*
> *terminating your very existence.*

Doing It Her Way

Amazon.com's Joy Covey was sick of school and dropped out her freshman year in high school. She returned to school, tested out and got her GED. From there she went to California State University at Fresno and nailed her CPA when she was 19-years-old. Bringing her smarts to Amazon landed her as its CFO. Jeff Bezos is a smart guy. Joy Covey is also smart . . . very. And, Bezos recognized her smarts. Working closely with him, she moved from CFO to being the Chief Strategy Officer.

When asked if her parents were upset in an interview in October 2000 with *FORTUNE*, (her father was a doctor and her mother a nurse), Covey said,

> My parents had a complete and utter disregard for social expectations. They knew it wouldn't do any good. I thought, they won't beat me or throw me out. If I don't obey, what can they do? I decided, there's no more following the rules.

It's well documented that bright kids get bored fast. Covey was no exception. A high-school dropout, who later tested for her GED, now holds advanced degrees from Harvard. She's working in a company that's a perfect example of doing things differently, of breaking the rules. By breaking society's expected rules—going to school the "traditional" way—she created the right fit for her. And, an excellent fit for amazon.com.

The Women's New Club

No single group of women illustrates the existence of outsiders as well as the women in the United States Senate. Two states have both their Senate positions held by women—California (Dianne Feinstein and Barbara Boxer) and Maine (Susan Collins and Olympia Snowe). Until 1989, only four women in America's history had been elected to full time Senate positions without succeeding their husbands who had died in office.

In 1996, Maryland's Democrat Senator Barbara Mikulski contacted Texas' Republican Senator Kay Bailey Hutchinson and basically said, "Let's get together." Her proposal was to create a joint effort to build relationships among the then nine female Senators. Being a Democrat or Republican didn't matter. In 2000, three more women joined them. First Lady Hillary Clinton was elected as the junior Senator from New York, Maria Cantwell in a close race in Washington and Missouri's Jean Caranhan stepped into her deceased husband's Senatorial seat won after he died in a plane crash campaigning for it.

The nine Senators have increased their numbers. They get together on a regular basis over dinner, inviting other prominent women leaders, such as Justice Sandra Day O'Connor, to join them. Their unwritten rules are fairly simple—nothing gets repeated outside of their dinners and no business is done, another rule breaker. These highly visible women have broken the assumed rules of partisanship within the Senate halls — they collaborate and have learned that no one has to do business 24/7.

The Vision Is Worthy

Entrepreneur and author Susan Stautberg is one of the new breeds of executives today. In the early seventies, she was a TV correspondent for a Westinghouse-owned station in Philadelphia and made a pitch at that time to open a bureau in Washington, D.C. Told "no" by the management at Westinghouse, she quit her job and set up a free-lance TV bureau in Washington the same year. Because of its location and the tenacity of Stautberg, the bureau got so many scoops for stations across the country that Westinghouse aggressively pursued her, hiring her back a year later . . . as head of its first Washington bureau.

After a few years, she decided it was time that she got an insider's view of government and from 1974 to 1975 she became a White House Fellow. During this time, she had the opportunity to work with then Vice President Nelson A. Rockefeller and Secretary of State Henry Kissinger. She later became head of communications at the U.S. Products Safety Commission, with a few more stops in between before landing her position as director of communications at Touche Ross in New York, which eventually led to the creation of a new publishing house. Today, she is CEO of PartnerCom Corporation in New York, a company that creates and manages Advisory Boards for prestigious corporations and organizations globally.

Because of her love for the written word and journalism, she began to write articles, which then led her to books. During that time, she experienced what most authors experience when they are out on the road promoting their books—there are none in the stores. She then began to think, "If I had a publishing company . . . The thought began to run through my mind. I raised close to $750,000 from investors and created Master-Media in New York."

After ten years, 125 published books and several best sellers later, Stautberg decided to shift gears once again, breaking the rules along the way. She's a firm believer in testing yourself—trying changes even if they don't work.

> Keep testing yourself. Career changes breed self-confidence. The key to confidence is to believe that you're in control. It is critical to learn that even if the doors shut, there's a window open, somewhere.

Stautberg has gone through a number of crises in her life both personally and professionally. When she decided to start MasterMedia, she was looking forty in the eye. She figured if she was going to fail at this age, she could still pick herself up, go back to "school" again and come out the door or window—certainly one more time. When she created her startup, conventional wisdom said that there was no way she could compete with the more established publishing houses.

> There are several reasons I reached out to raise the money to start my own publishing house. Certainly, I

experienced a number of things that publishers don't do for their authors and I felt if I failed to succeed, I could pick myself up. Nothing ventured, nothing gained. I also felt that women as a whole were not raised to ask for money. It would be a good experience—I had to do it. The vision was worthy.

One thing I didn't realize was how hard the work really was. It takes many years for most companies to finally get going, and even after four years the majority of small companies only hire a few employees. I am one of those people that hate the term "if only." If only I had done this, if only I had done that. I believe that it's better to try it. I have never had the regret that comes from not trying something.

I had the pleasure of being one of Stautberg's authors. We did three books together. She broke every rule of traditional publishing and her authors cheered her on. She understood how to work with the media; she understood the value of coupling publishing with authors who were speakers; she understood that in order to succeed, she had to create a partnership with corporations and authors. When MasterMedia ceased publishing, it was a loss for all—Stautberg, her authors, and the public.

Fly with the Eagles
The adage, "If you want to be an eagle, you must fly with eagles" is as old as I can remember. Today, most of us get our info from the tube—TV. Although viewers have reduced their patronage of the Big Three—NBC, ABC and CBS, dozens of other channels have surfaced that have garnered viewers. Upstarts just a few years

ago, CNN, ESPN, CNBC, CNNfn, FOX, HBO, OXYGEN and many more, have created a major dent in the revenues generated via advertising on popular, and not so popular shows. They each broke the rules when they decided to buck the norm, and so did viewers. No longer were the Big Three the only source to be trusted with newsworthy news and entertainment.

The first lady of television was Lucille Ball—on the screen and behind it. Finally, someone has stepped in to remind and reinforce the power of women in the media. Oprah Winfrey arrived. Today, with her Harpo Productions, her highly rated daily show, Oprah's Book Club that has skyrocketed dozens of works to bestseller hood, producing projects such as the Emmy winning *Oprah Winfrey Presents Tuesdays with Morrie*, the launching of *O: The Oprah Magazine*—a sell out on its first day on the newsstands and most successful magazine launch in history, a philanthropist with her Angel Network creating millions of dollars in scholarships to being a pivotal point for both Al Gore and George W. Bush in their drives for the Presidency in 2000, Oprah is a hurricane force wherever she lands.

In my mind there is no one else who has the wherewithal, which can match her savvy, moxie and guts. Has everything she touched turned to gold? No, most likely she would point out the failure of her movie *Beloved* was painful. I believed that the sting she felt with the *Beloved* project became a cosmic goose for her. Here she was, the Queen of self-help, advising others to get their act together and to grow from their failures, experiencing an overload of public rejection—i.e., they love my show, why not my beloved *Beloved*?

The golden egg came in the form of partnerships. She teamed up with Hearst Magazines and *O* was birthed. An incredible success that Martha Steward would envy.

If you were to observe her, on her show, working on her myriad of productions, you would note that she surrounds herself with people who are really, really good— from her executive producer to support staff—Oprah wants the best. She's willing to bend, and break the rules in her drive to be the best.

The Frippy Way

Patricia Fripp was born in England. She arrived in America with her styling shears, minimal funds, and an unlimited bank of energy and determination in the seventies. Fripp was to become one of San Francisco's most successful men's hair stylists, eventually opening her own salon.

In the eighties, she sold it to embark upon her next full-time career—in the world of professional speaking. She is recognized as one of the best motivators in the industry, keynoting conventions and conferences worldwide and teaching others how to do what she does well. As the Millennium dawned, she birthed another career, as a professional speaking coach to aspiring speakers and executives worldwide.

Fripp believes that to be the best, you have to reach for it. And that reaching includes surrounding yourself with the winners of life and being willing to be different from what is considered the standard way of doing things.

When I first went into the men's hairstyling business, I went into it as I do everything—100 percent. I was working six days a week, twelve hours a day, going out every evening, passing out my business cards.

I had been trained by Jay Sebring and noticed from him that it doesn't matter how good you are at anything, the world has to know. I went on radio shows and television shows and had write-ups in all the local papers about my work, about myself as a successful entrepreneur. We had a woman come work with us a couple of years after all this relative success came my way. I realized it must be a bit overwhelming for her, as I was so obviously the star in the salon.

To help her build her confidence, and customer base, I tried to get her involved in things and give her my overflow business. One day, a gentleman from a local radio show came in to interview me to see if I could fill up an hour radio talk show. I said, 'Judy, you come talk to him, tell him your point of view.'

After we had been talking for a while, he said, 'Patricia, you have been very successful, do other people in your industry resent your success?' Without a moment's hesitation I said, 'Well, of course not, why would anyone resent my success when they see how hard I work.' At exactly the same moment, without a second's hesitation, Judy said, 'Well, of course they resent her success, they don't care what she does to get it.'

That was one of the greatest realizations of my entire life. I have always believed in such a Walt Disney world, where everything was the way I assumed it was supposed to be. It never occurred to me anyone would be envious or anyone would hold it against me or resent it or try and backstab me. That was the turning point at which I made the decision I have to be very careful about my associates. From that day on, I made the conscious choice to associate only with winners in my own industry and other industries.

A lot of this came from when I was growing up. My brother was so brilliant, always top of the class and considered by many a genius in the music industry. Although people did not expect much of girls in those days, I got the feeling I was not as smart as other people so I never missed school. I received 100 percent attendance certificates for years. Never won anything else, but always got a certificate saying I turned up every day.

Turning up every day led to the development of exceptionally good work habits. When I became an apprentice hairdresser and we would practice on models, all the other girls would do one or two, I would do five, and then go home and practice on the neighbors. All the other hairstylists thought lunch hours were for eating lunch. I thought lunch hours were for squeezing in three extra customers. My boss told me I made 30 percent more income for the salon than the guys that in fact were more experienced and better hairstylists. When I came to America, I could not believe that I started at 50 percent commission. My boss used to say, 'If you go to England and bring over twenty-eight of your friends, I will be a multimillionaire.' I always responded, 'Charles, I don't know twenty-eight people in England that work like me.'

Patricia Fripp broke the rules when she first started in her hair styling business by doing so much more that the other stylists; she broke the rules in the association business by becoming the first woman to be president of the National Speakers Association where men had always held the top slot; she broke the rules in the speaking business by being one of the most sought after speakers with speaking bureaus where men had ruled for so long; she broke the rules when she spun off her speaking skills to teach executives how to grab, influence and motivate their audiences and personnel. Fripp wouldn't be where she is today, if she had followed the rules.

Keeper #7
As a rule breaker, it's important
to make sure you know some people who are
as confident as you—or even more so,
because they are going to be there to
support you as well as provide you with a
model for confident behavior. They will also
be your cheerleaders as you break through
a variety of barriers in your journey.

Chapter Five

Step #4

Keep on Learning . . . The Power of Renewal

I didn't see its relevance, its magnitude, the way I should have.

Jack Welch,
CEO, GE on the Internet, 1999

When my first book, *The Woman's Guide to Financial Savvy, was* published in 1981, 1 had no idea that I could/would write, much less write several additional books. Nor did I know at that time that this would become my passion and vocation. Twenty plus years later, I am writing several monthly columns and creating at least one new book a year. At the same time, I am always focusing on the next project and reading a multitude of others' books. Why? To learn something new.

There is always something that you don't know and

now is a great time to go after it. Learn something. Prove to yourself you can master it. Become an expert at it. Of course, you may never become an expert in it, but you'll become an expert to yourself. Who knows? You just may become a master, able to turn your newly gained knowledge into a tangible asset.

It is an extraordinary event when mastering something is achieved within a short period of time. Most likely, the "something" will have to be repeated many, many times before true mastery can be obtained. And, because of our rapidly evolving environment, many things mastered may be obsolete within a short period of time—possibly even before you have mastered it! If you hang on to the past, the ways of doing things that you have done for decades, the future could sidestep you.

You should be dedicated to constantly learning and stretching yourself with the idea of doing a little better than what was expected. Find something new. Learn about it, accomplish it, and move on. It's critical to acquire the tools to work with. If you are insecure about the way you make speeches or presentations, take a course. If you need to speak a foreign language and don't do it terribly well, go out and get trained in it. If you can't manage money very well, get a pro to coach you. Stretching and learning new things is just part of taking care of business. Taking care of you. All of us have what it takes when we need it; we just need to be committed to going about doing it.

Even Old Horses Learn New Tricks
GE's legendary CEO Jack Welch confessed to not jumping on the communications bandwagon that has be-

come the mainstream throughout the world—email—in a timely manner. His wife had used the Internet for several years before he finally went surfing in early 1999 . . . for the first time! She introduced him to Yahoo! Investor sites where people were grumbling, complaining or cheering about GE. Welch was hooked.

He has shared his introduction to the 24/7 world in extensive interviews with numerous business magazine. In the January 1, 2001 issue of *Newsweek*, he shares his reaction to those Internet postings—

> . . . Jack's a jerk. Jack's great. Jack should do this. My God, it was fascinating. So I started sneaking in from the pool during the rest of the vacation to look at it. When I got home, I bought a CD-ROM and spent a weekend learning how to type. It gave you a contest: "You've now got 21 words a minute." So I spent weekends competing at it. I can type pretty well now.

During the many weeks he sat himself down with the computer to learn how to type, Welch saw an incredible opportunity at his, and everyone else's, fingertips within the GE empire.

> . . . it didn't grab me with the intensity it should have. I didn't see its relevance, its magnitude, the way I should have. Finally there came a point where I was being hit on all sides with it. It didn't take a genius at that point.

Jack Welch's "aha" is creating a revolution in GE. From managing the business more efficiently to saving over a $100 million in travel related expenses. GE's online sales are in the billions today and will only grow. Welch feels that only the tip of the iceberg has been scratched via the Internet. Where Welch plans on retiring within a year, he has continued to search and learn out new things and concepts for the benefit of his company, and himself, including being a good typer.

Get Back On

PartnerCom CEO Susan Stautberg feels it is important to do *something new* and something that might make you a little nervous.

> One of my steps would be to do something—something that might make you a little nervous or that you might think is too big a risk. Go out and try it. Believe in yourself through thick and thin. If you fail, just pick yourself up. It is the hardest thing to do after all the failures or when you are turned down for something time after time. You've got to pick yourself up and try again.
>
> It's like falling of a horse the first time. If you don't get back on, it's so hard to get back on in the future. But if you get back on the first time you make the fall, then you learn to get back on and try again no matter how many times you fall. You pick yourself up and leave the door and go look for a different window.
>
> It's also important to realize that it is not always going to be perfect. Not everyone is going to be treated alike, but you have to tell yourself inside that you can do it. A confident voice needs to come up within

you that tells you to push onward no matter how bad times are. When you try something and learn something new, it allows you to find new windows.

The Past, the Present and the Future is at Your Fingertips

Years ago, I had dinner with science fiction writer Ray Bradbury. He told me that his idea of the ideal education for all kids would be to lock them in the public library and let them out when they are 18! He firmly believed that it would solve problems and educate them at the same time. I added that it would most likely create a few problems as well.

In the past ten years, I've spoken with and interviewed thousands of successful men and women. One of their commonalities is that they read—not just one or two books, but dozens each year. And, they shared that they don't keep to the business area, non-fiction club— they read books of which many are purely fictional.

Executive coach Pat Goss if firmly rooted in Silicon Valley. She is a strong believer in learning all the time. Her career has included professorship, aerospace communicator, human resource director for a multi-billion dollar corporation to executive coach. Throughout the 20 plus years that I've known her, she has consistently had at least two books being read/devoured on an ongoing basis.

I think that it is important that everyone read to keep current so they know what's going on in their particular industry or in an industry or group they want to move into. I have also found it important to read biographies. A lot of people think that biographies are boring, but they aren't. They are written about people who have accomplished things. You are able to get a sense of what their strengths and weaknesses are and maybe you will even be able to relate to them. And what you end up finding out as you read biography after biography is that there are several multiple traits that are common amongst them.

People are often amazed when I do or repeat something and they ask, 'Well, how did you get that information?' When I tell them that I read it in a book about a particular individual they are always surprised. It is also interesting to note the variety of things that people who lack confidence in themselves and haven't succeeded have in common, too. I am a firm believer in anyone and everybody reading a lot.

Failing is Learning Too!

Some of the greatest learning comes from failure, which comes in all kinds of sizes and shapes. One failure is not recognizing you may be the wrong fit—that the situation you are in, or you work at, is wrong—all wrong. Of the thousands of men and women that I have interviewed, the great majority will say, in reflection, that they should have gotten out sooner.

One former college professor shared,

Intelligent persistence is usually a good thing, but not always. In my case, I was totally tuned out to the politics of my campus. I was so focused on achieving my own personal goals that I didn't recognize/ acknowledge the deterioration of the changing positions of the college I headed a major department in.

I had created a collaboration with the Dean of the Business School that awarded a double degree (engineering and business) to students participating in the program. When the Dean took another position out-of-state, I worked hard to continue the program. What I didn't realize was that my key supporter was gone. I became orphaned, making it almost impossible to continue and grow the program. Within a year of Jim's departure, my entire department was eliminated. What a shock!

When circumstances change, it is always smart to step back and assess what is happening. Too often, you are too close to the situation. It's hard to see, or learn anything, when you become myopic in your quest.

Even at the Top, Learning is #1

Men and women who work within the government must keep their ears and eyes open. They also must keeping learning new things. Being fearful is not exclusive to those who are not in the public eye. Arts advocate and former second lady, Joan Mondale shares a story about Rosalynn Carter.

I think the Rosalynn Carter example of being very shy and forcing herself to speak is a very clear example of someone who said, 'I'm going to do this. My husband has confidence in me, I have to do it. I am not going to be left by the wayside.'

Mondale also shared a story about Washington DC in general. It's a fast moving pace; many of the women she knew were married to men who carried a high profile within the government. And, who too often, were left behind out of fear and not learning new things.

> There are women who don't grow and those are the
> sad ones. And sometimes those are the ones that are
> left behind. Their husbands grow professionally.
> They are left there. Some are alone and still married,
> others are divorced. It is very sad. I have seen
> that in two cases with friends who have lost their
> husbands as their careers grew and blossomed.
>
> My friends were frightened and afraid. They
> wouldn't go with them, travel with them, they were
> fearful of airplanes and all the hazards and
> excitement of travel. They were very conservative
> and afraid of change. Eventually, their marriages
> broke up.

The Trainer has to Learn

Texas based Joe Charbonneau has trained hundreds of thousands of men and women on achieving professional excellence. One of his mottoes is tied directly in to learning something new versus floating about in the status quo.

> If you ease up, everything else goes down. Bear in mind
> that you can only coast down, never up. That affects
> you as a person, as a parent, on the job, as a friend, and
> as a professional. Climbing downhill is a snap. It's the

steps as we try something new, stretch, and move up in our environments that leave their mark.

The Lessons He Learned

Catching up with piled up reading on a vacation in Hawaii, I came across the September 2000 issue of *Golf Digest*. In it was an insightful interview with megastar Tiger Woods. He was asked to share what he has learned over the last few years. Now, keep in mind that he's golf's billion-dollar dude. When he turned pro in 1996, Woods did not know how to access his money. Oh, he admits to signing contracts and cashing a few checks. But, he was clueless in how to activate a credit card! Here's what he shared,

> Some people think I was born into riches, but that's far from the truth. I had never owned a credit card. Never needed one. However, I learned quickly. I also learned how to manage my money and account for every dime. I am determined not to be like so many other professional athletes who can't read a balance sheet. I've learned that attention to detail in business is as important as it is in major championships.

Woods continues that his education has taken plenty of twists and turns. From what type of playing schedule fits him mentally and physically to what he should be (and not be) eating to how to work with the media and the golf public. But, he says that his most important learning curve has been in the people department—

relationships. Trust is essential. When someone is as high profiled as Tiger Woods is, having the right person/group in your circle is critical. They support, cheer and add to one's core values. Woods says,

Thankfully, I'm still learning.

As we all should be.

Keeper #8
The person you are, and choose to become will be based on the books you read and people you meet. Learning something new keeps you mentally alive and alert. Your new motto is: Thou Shall Be Dedicated to Constantly Learning!

Learning something new will increase your confidence level by the sheer fact that you will master or expand in an area that you know little or nothing about. Just as a child takes pride in her accomplishments— whether it's learning to tie shoes, a new song, mastering a spelling list, or painting a "work of art," so will you. Learning something new is like taking on a challenge of an old foe and winning. With each new experience, each new win, you continue to stretch yourself and your mind, it rejuvenator of the brain cells. Definitely, a healthy way to live.

Chapter Six

Step #5

You're Never Alone . . . Going Solo Is for Sissies

When my partner died, there was no one to check with. I was alone and it frightened me. I lost my confidence.

Carole Hyatt
Author, *Shifting Gears* and *When Smart People Fail*

As a mother, I have experienced tremendous joy and pain with the four children that I have had. My two daughters have active lives, with Shelley working for a large company in a field that was foreign to her, even throughout college as it is to me today. Visiting her twice a year, I'm always interested to hear what's going on in space—she's the project manager for the Hubble Telescope.

My younger daughter, Sheryl, worked with me for

several years before branching out into other areas. She's also working in a field that she never thought she would be in—health insurance for high-risk individuals. She's also the mother of the apple of my eye, grandson Frank, now an energetic teen.

My two sons died. Billy, when he was a baby, and Frank, when he was nineteen years old. At both times I felt alone—isolated. . The overcoming of that aloneness was handled in different ways. When Billy died, I was twenty-five years old and had really not been around death much. I had never experienced the death of children. Children aren't supposed to die before their parents do. I dealt with my pain by becoming a hermit. I isolated myself in a room and painted for hours—listening to music—and emerged from my cocoon several months later, ready to cope and reach out once again to the world.

During that time a friend, an older woman had visited me. She left with me a small medallion; on it was the Serenity Prayer. The prayer that says, "God, give me the courage to face the things that come. To change what I can. The serenity to accept what's unchangeable, and the wisdom to know the difference." All critical ingredients to living. The effect of Billy's death hit me the most when my son Frank, seven years old, raced up the stairs to finally hold his longed-for brother.

Twelve years later, death was at my doorstep once again. Frank was nineteen. An accident. Only this time, I didn't have the luxury of withdrawing to a cocoon and painting my way out. This time, the news of the accident had been on the radio, on the television, and in the press.

This time, I reached out to people I knew in the media to help knock down an old bridge that had been deserted—a bridge that should have been knocked down when a new one had been built alongside of it. This time, when Frank died, I didn't feel as isolated as when Billy died. When Billy died, I was young and inexperienced and certainly immature as to what happens and how one feels when there is death and the depth of sadness that surrounds self and family. I didn't really have anyone to turn to who had walked through the journey that I was thrust into. None of my friends knew what to do with me. None of them had experienced a baby dying. No one ever suggested that I should get some therapy to help me move along or to find the groups that are out there to support mothers and families when loved ones die.

When Frank died, things were different. Friends swooped in to help. Certainly, we were all a lot older and a lot more experienced in life. I felt a commitment to reach out to others, to Frank's ten friends who were there when he fell. To help them along in their grief and at the same time, helping myself. There were support groups out there that I could tap into, that I could absorb and gather strength from to help me move on. With all that, it still took me a year to really feel I had strength. It wasn't something that happened instantly.

There were times that I felt so alone and yet, with my eyes and ears open, I learned and knew that there was hundreds of mothers in my own community that had had children die. I was definitely not alone.

No matter what you are going through that has knocked your confidence down, you are not alone.

Whether it's a job, whether it's a personal problem, whether it's an appearance or an upbringing factor or a divorce, or death, or any of life's problems that land at our feet, you're not alone. There are thousands who have walked and will walk in the shoes that you're currently in. And although the pain that you're feeling can be so intense and so deep, bear in mind that you're not that unique, you're not that alone. The Lone Ranger does not exist anymore.

Reaching Out

Jean Hollands is the President and CEO of the Growth & Leadership Center in the heart of Silicon Valley. She has worked with all the major companies in the Valley, from the Executive branch to staff support. Hollands has been featured internationally on career issues and has written several best-selling books. She's known as someone with the magic wand—getting to the heart of a matter in minutes and working toward a resolution and solution with her clients.

When Hollands was newly widowed in the nineties, her confidence was at a low point. At this time, her entire staff did an evaluation on her and discovered that all her scores were miserably low. In Jean's words,

> Mind you, I teach coaching to executives and have been in the careers field for 25 years. How could I flunk my own subjects? I was known as a micromanager and one who blew up when I was passionate about something.
>
> I was mortified with how my staff felt. Here I was, beloved by my corporate clients, heralded by

the press, but my own staff thought I was a controlling bully some of the time. I felt hurt and despondent.

The only thing I could do was take my own medicine. I asked for help from my staff. Of course, I went to grief counseling about my husband's death and I came to realize that his loss prevented me from accepting any even small loss very well. So, I unconsciously wanted to be in charge of every decision and could not let anything go easily.

My staff gave me feedback on a regular basis and I checked myself when I was about to present one of my passionate diatribes. This took discipline. I learned to distract my passion to positive areas and not to concentrate on what didn't go right on what my staff did not do according to my demands or wishes.

Hollands' advise is that when your confidence bursts, you have to remind yourself that it is only temporary, not a permanent affliction. She feels that you must tap into your supportive friends and colleagues. She adds,

It's smart for you to you line up all your supportive friends and colleagues and ask them to assure you, to give you the good news about you. Then, ask for feedback about the current dilemma you are in. Instead of making excuses for the way you do things, make a deliberate attempt to discipline yourself to change. Inside you are still the same old wonderful self. You are just adding to your repertoire, and that's just a bonus!

Jean Hollands firmly believes that everything starts with confidence—leadership, teamsmanship, even relationships with others. Your ultimate happiness and tranquility begins and ends with your love, understanding and acceptance of self.

Losing Part of Self

Everything was going great for author and market researcher Carole Hyatt. She and her partner had a growing business in New York City with forty employees on their payroll. Hyatt thought that she had always been self-reliant. Certainly, her best-selling books, *The Woman's' Selling Game, When Smart People Fail,* and *Shifting Gears,* were spawned on her self-reliance. Everything seemed to be perfect. Perfect, that is, until her partner died unexpectantly. Until then, the business was going well and she was in great demand as a speaker and a best-selling author.

> We were a couple, a business couple. She had her areas of strength and I had my areas of strength. We made our decisions as a couple, we rehearsed as a couple, there was always a person to go and try things out on to build confidence with.
>
> I've always said that one plus one equals ten. In actuality, eleven. It does not equal two, it definitely equals eleven, and it is eleven because you have that confidence of another person behind you—you have that other mind. You have the accountability—you have someone who has been with you as your partner who understands your shorthand. I didn't under-

stand that until after my partner died-it was a post-evaluation.

And I've always felt that partnerships are better than being alone. But partnerships, like all marriages, have their inconveniences, too. You can't do things solo, you can't make unilateral decisions—you can't if you are sharing a staff, just decide that a staff member is going to do this or that. You have to plan it together as a partnership. There are always pros and cons.

During our eighteen-year partnership, I would sometimes want to run off and do XYZ, she didn't want to do XYZ, so we would have to negotiate as you would in a marriage. Sometimes that would irritate me. I would want to go off on the spur of the moment and do it, she was more reasoning. When she died, it was clear that there was no one to check with anymore and that scared me. It frightened me and I lost my confidence.

I did not believe that I could continue to run a market and social behavior research company. Making the payroll week after week frightened me. I didn't think I could handle all the clients; there was no one there to be a buffer. There was no one to discuss things with, there was no one to understand the business the way she understood it.

Although I had very well meaning employees, they were never privy to the whole business. We had, many different parts of the business and I lost my sense of self, my confidence, and my ability to make decisions. I ran scared. Then, I determined to close the company—to sell it as quickly as I could.

I went out and found a buyer and sold it within three months.

I then came home and literally did not do anything new for a year. I did some of the old things, I just wouldn't stretch, and I couldn't do anything new. I lost my creativity. I lost my sense of exploration. I lost my sense of adventure. I thought I would never do anything new again. I was doomed to repeat the same old things. I felt so fake.

Groups would hire me to do the woman's selling game seminar, which was highly motivational. I would get out of my nightgown, put on my good-looking designer suits, put on my makeup, and get on the plane. When I arrived, I was picked up by all these excited people who would be jumping up and down and then I'd get on stage and go into automatic. Rah! Rah! Rah!

And, then, I would wonder where that was coming from because I didn't feel that way and I kept thinking this must be very hollow for those who are here. I felt like an actress putting on a mask. The costume and the makeup would go on. The key was turned. I would smile and I would say all the right things and I guess they were okay. It was so well rehearsed, I had done the script so many times that I could go into automatic. Then I would get back on the plane, take off the makeup, take off the suit, come home, put on the nightgown, and crawl back into bed. I did this for a full year.

I didn't know what was happening to me. I just had a sense of a loss of self-esteem, self-confidence, and self-creativity. And then a friend came to visit me. She had just been fired from a job. And as she spoke, everything she said sounded so familiar. I said, 'Yes, I know. In fact, I think we have experienced the same thing, but we arrived at it by different routes.' We both felt a lack of self-confidence, esteem, in her case money. Everything sounded so familiar. She said, 'How could that be? You sold your company and I got fired.'

As I thought about it, it was the same thing because we both had had a loss. We both were in mourning. As part of that, our confidence was lost. Finally, I told my friend that this was a process. I think we just have to go through this process, through the mourning. Maybe what we need to do is to talk about it-to share about it, that's what support groups are for. In Judaism, there is a period of one year where you go to temple every morning. Death is never discussed, rather, the continuation of life.

Her fired friend was Linda Gottlieb. The book *When Smart People Fail* was created from that initial visit. Beginning with their personal stories (and hundreds of others, they tell the depth of what crises and failure can do; how these hundreds of brave men and women over-came them and reinvented themselves. When Hyatt spoke with Gottlieb, it became the catalyst for her to move on. She realized what had happened to her had also happened to her friend. In effect, Hyatt was ahead of her in her awareness and her growth. Hyatt believes that there are triggers in life, things that trigger us into the next stage. Her having lunch with Gottlieb was the trigger that opened the door for her to move on.

Slow Superstars

Two superstars share a common disability—one's the highest paid lawyer in America; the other's the CEO of the quintessential Internet company.

David Boies charges anywhere from $0 to $750 an hour at this writing. When working for the U.S. Government in the Microsoft case, he charged $40 an hour as he shredded witness after witness; in representing Al Gore in the Florida recount fiasco, he worked pro-bono; when recently won cases involving price fixing are finally distributed, his firm stands to net over $60 million. Not bad for someone who couldn't read until the third grade.

John Chambers, Cisco's CEO ranks with the top CEOs in the world—including GE's Jack Welch who invited Chambers to speak at one of GE's management meetings. At one of Cisco's Take Our Daughters to Work events, surprised employees learned that their CEO had a disability. When a little girl tried to speak to some of the employees during the event, she teared up and said that she had a learning disability. Chambers immediately noted her discomfort. He jumped up to comfort her. He told her, and the hundreds of employees who were there that he too had a learning disability. And, that when he was growing up, kids routinely made fun of him.

Two men, superstars in their respective professions, each ridiculed and sometimes alone when they were kids found ways to get around their disabilities, Chambers learned to work hard to get around and through his. Boies did the same, tapping into an incredible memory that enabled him to accelerate just about anything that he takes on, including being a wiz at cards.

Getting Stung

Nutrition advocates and executives of Hillestad Pharmaceutical, Don and Lucy Hillestad have had more than their share of hard knocks. The Hillestad family "school of hard knocks" has ranged from being laughed at and told that they are quacks when they first started in the nutritional field to being set up in a sting operation in a small town.

That sting operation eventually lead nowhere, all charges were dropped. It was discovered that the individuals behind the operation were corrupt and had been leading the authorities up the wrong tree. Before that happened, hundreds of thousands of dollars were spent on their defense. Their good name had been smeared in the television, radio, and the print medias for months on end. Says Lucy Hillestad,

> Even today, after everything we have gone through, I can look around and see people who have had much, much worse things happen to them than what has happened to us. In my own small way, I feel that I can rise above these tragedies of life and a lot of the things that are going to continue to happen to us.
>
> The unfortunate part of being involved in those charges is that not only did it hurt us politically, but also it hurt us professionally and financially. Many people believed what they read and heard in the media. From then on, even after all charges were

dropped and the state admitted that the chief witness had perjured himself forty-one times, people were very skeptical about doing business with us.

One of the hardest things for us that happened was many people who we thought were friends turned out not to be friends. There are times that we felt alone, and then our real friends and new friends rallied around us to support us and stand by us.

Coming from the Wrong Side

Of all the people that I have interviewed, the one that I have the most parallel life experiences with is Leslie Charles. She wasn't known always as Leslie Charles. She started out in life as Connie Allen. She later became Connie Allen Kuripla. She grew up in Michigan on the west side of Lansing—my early years were in Los Angeles, California. She had married at sixteen—so had I. She had had three kids by the time she was twenty— so had I. She had gone through her divorce in her mid-twenties—so had I. She had made $350 a month in 1969—so had I. She had had an adult son die—so had I. As we spent several hours in the airport in Phoenix, Arizona, I felt as if I were listening to an echo.

After her divorce, she worked as a secretary. She hated the job. She hated working. She didn't really want to work. Instead she was just waiting for a nice guy to come along and marry her kids and her—the expected thing for a woman born on the west side of Lansing.

At the end of two and a half years, she found herself disenchanted with where she was heading. Then the light bulb turned on. She recognized that she had no goals and she really wasn't doing anything for herself. She didn't know what she wanted, she only knew what she didn't want, and she didn't want to have to continue as she was.

So she quit her job and got unemployment insurance. She figured in she was already destitute—a little bit less money wasn't going to make any difference and she could spend more time with her kids, trying to figure out who she was and where she wanted to go next. Leslie shares,

> During this time, I worked on my tan (in those days, traumas were easier to take with a good tan!), played with my kids, and one of my friends said, 'Gee, it's a shame you are not on public assistance because if you were, they've got a program that would put you through school.' I had told my friend about my desire to finish my high school diploma, that I felt really inferior without that education. I was scared to death that I would finally meet someone who would think I was really neat and then the minute that he found out that I didn't have any degree, he wouldn't talk to me.
>
> So I studied a little, got my GED with the scores arriving on my twenty-ninth birthday. I had passed everything except math. I took my scores to the Department of Social Services and said, 'I want help, I want to improve my life.' I walked out of there with food stamps in my pockets as Lansing's newest welfare mother. The following fall I started school at the local community college. In 1970, I made the honor roll!

This was my new beginning—the doors really started to open for me. I loved school and did well. I even took two terms of music literature, studying classical music as well as the basics.

I graduated from Lansing Community College with an associate degree in business-in those days, that meant glorified secretarial work. I also completed a certificated program for library technology. My rationale at that time was that I liked books. I liked to read. The end result was I got a job as a supervisor in the library at Lansing Community College just before I graduated.

I had a party when I went off welfare to celebrate my reentrance into society. Invitations were sent out. They said, 'The children of Connie L. Kuripla invite you to celebrate her reentry into society.'

Five years had passed since my divorce; *he* had not shown up and *he* was the person I was waiting for to find the kids and me. It finally dawned on me that I may have to work for a long time; that I need to start thinking about a real career. I want to make more money and grow as a person at the same time.

A friend worked at Xerox and suggested I interview as a sales rep. I blew my first interview. They asked me a series of questions: Why Xerox? Why you? Why sales? I couldn't really answer them. I thought about it, pepped myself up, and two months later went back. Xerox hired me! A real job—this was a quantum leap for Connie Kuripla. I was a sales rep. I wore a business suit. People from the west side of Lansing didn't wear business suits.

This was my smoking, drinking time . . . and I

was a terrific pool player. By becoming a good pool player, I could still talk to men, have a good time, and if I decided that I wanted to dance with them, I could make that decision. Then I met a man who was a few years younger than me and was different from most of the others. We've been together 25 years now.

I stayed at Xerox for two years, not doing anything really great. I quit my job, considered going back on unemployment and back to school. My objective was to finish my bachelor's degree. My family was always 100 percent supportive. Neighbors were critical, but *never* my family.

One day, the program coordinator at the Seminar Center with Management Development at Lansing Community College asked me about my background. I told him I had been on welfare for almost three years, but had pulled off it when I went back to work. Then he asked me what I was currently doing and I said, 'Funny, I have just quit my job.' He offered a part-time job at $10 an hour.

It was during this time that I started reading, I started doing things—I was having fun, I was getting paid for it, stopped drinking, stopped smoking, and I was making over $20,000 a year. Huge bucks for me. The Seminar Center grew, I became one of the senior trainers and as my expertise grew, so did my stress.

Going to the supervisor, I said that conditions were not good and if they did not improve, I would quit. As those words tumbled out of my mouth, I knew that I could be in trouble. Although I was their senior core trainer, a major client was the state of

Michigan and I still didn't have my bachelor's degree—I did not qualify to do contract work for them.

I had two calls asking for me specifically to do a program for different clients. I told them that if they were interested in having me, to call me in two weeks. I gave them my home number and told them I had just quit. They called. Those two calls were from the American Institute of Banking and the Public Service Commission, a state agency. The time was November 1979. I had $3,000 in the bank, a guarantee of $1,600 in earnings for 1980. With my savings, I bought an IBM typewriter, an answering machine, and started my business. Those two phone calls seeded my business.

In her growing-up days, Charles says that she had such low self-esteem as a child that she didn't think anything positive could happen. She began to think about having another name. She didn't want to hold on to her married name, Kuripla, or her maiden name, Allen.

One day, a friend made up the name of Leslie Meredith Charles. My life partner, Rob, loved it and started calling me that. As a joke, I started using the name Charles to order dinner reservations and pizzas, any time that you would give a name instead of my *real* name of Kuripla. I even took Leslie Charles as a DBA for my company.

When I came up with situations that I didn't know whether I could handle or not, I would ask myself how would Leslie handle it? In effect, Leslie

Charles became my alter ego. In 1982, I changed my name legally to Leslie Charles.

Leslie Charles was able to look back at the upbringing of Connie Allen, remove herself, and move into a new environment, a new society in which both she and her children matured. Leslie Charles did not have a positive upbringing. Rather, she had to literally rebirth herself, start over and bring herself up. Her latest birthing? The book, *Why is Everyone So Cranky?*

Keeper #9
No matter what the situation is, you are not alone. Most likely, thousands, even millions, have walked on your path before you.

You Are Not Alone

The most important point to keep in mind is that you are not alone and that every one of us is an important spoke in the wheel. The following is a small essay that has been printed several places and has no known author—I first saw it ten plus years ago—it was recently re-circulated via email. Its title is *Am I Really Needed?* The fact is all of us are needed, each of us counts. Keep it and reread it to remind yourself.

Xvxn though my typxwritxr is an old modxl, it works wxll xxcxpt for onx of thx kxys. I'vx wishxd many days that it workxd pxrfxctly. Trux, thxrx arx forty-two kxys that function, but onx kxy not working makxs thx difxrxncx.

Sonixtlmxs, it sxxms to mx that our organization is somxwhat likx my typxwritxr-not all thx pxoplx arx working propxrly. You might say, "Wxll, I'm only onx pxrson, it won't makx much diffxrxncx." But you sxx an organization, to bx xfficixnt, nxxds thx activx participation of xvxry pxrson. Thx nxxt time you think your xfforts arxn't nxxdxd, rxmxmbxr my typxwritxr, and say to yoursxlf, "I am a kxy pxrson and thxy nxxd mx vxry much."

Small things can be a big deal, the missing ingredi-ent. If isolated, hardly noticed; when included and sup-ported, an important link.

Chapter Seven

Step #6

Failure Is Not Your Enemy . . . It Happens

I have a friend who begins each day by standing in front of the mirror announcing, "I forgive you, kid " it's a sweet foolish nothing for moving on from yesterday's mistakes. After all, this is not a forced march—the point is to laugh along the way.

Diane Sawyer, ABC News

Feeling alone, and failing go hand-in-hand. Surveyed respondents were asked what kind of failures they had endured. The top two were being fired or laid off and the ending of a long-term relationship—primarily marriage. Endings have similarities. Often, there is disbelief—this can't be happening; often there is anger—I'll show him or her; often there is emotional distress—it's impossible to hold anything together; often, there's a rationalization—it's not my fault/problem, he or she is the problem/ trouble; and often, it's terminated privately—just you and the other person. Imagine what's it like when millions get to share in your agony.

We asked our respondents if they forgave themselves when they made mistakes. Men and women were close in this area where 19% of the men and 18% of the women said that they *always* did. More men than women were inclined to say that they *often* did with 51% reporting versus 42% of the women. Women were more inclined to report that they *sometimes* forgave them with 35% reporting and 25% of the men stating so. Finally, it was a tie with 5% of each saying that they *rarely* forgave themselves.

A Public Affair

Politics usually create interesting scenarios. If someone had written the script of the national election of 2000— few would have believed what happened could have happened. To my knowledge, no one was fired on camera. That script was used up in 1980. Karen Kessler was the executive director of Democratic Finance. She was fired on the floor of the Democratic Convention with a live mike and camera focused at her.

In 1980, I was the executive director for the New York area of the Democratic National Committee. I had been working for three and a half years building an entire operation for the party. After Walter Mondale was nominated at the Democratic Convention that summer, his staff decided that they were going to have their own people in the New York office. I was fired on the floor of the convention.

The reason I was given was he just wanted his own people. I was devastated. I thought I was working for the benefit of us all. I was under the belief that if you were good, you were rewarded.

A number of people sent telegrams to people and made phone calls on my behalf. My bosses said, 'We are not going to take this lying down.' Eventually, I was reinstated. I became very disenchanted with politics in general. My feelings were ambivalent about the Mondale staff since I wasn't really sure to what extent he was involved in these kinds of decisions.

What compounded the whole situation was that within five minutes of being told that my office was going to be changing gears, the media stuck a camera and a microphone in my face and said, 'We just heard the Mondale campaign is going to initiate a series of firings. We are with who we hear is the first of those firings.' I stood there sort of bug-eyed. My immediate thought, 'I hope my parents aren't watching.' It was absolutely devastating. My response to the interviewer was, 'I don't know what you are talking about,' and just sort of ran out.

What I did then was to fight it. It took me a little bit of time. I went back to my hotel room and sat down by myself for about three hours and then I started making phone calls until I began to feel that it was really unfair what I had been put through. That it really had nothing to do with who I was, for I knew that I had performed well. I knew that I was good at what I was doing. I knew that it wasn't right what had happened. So, in making these phone calls, I began to see if there wasn't some way that we could apply enough external pressure to people who were making these decisions. Possibly, the decision could be reversed.

And that's what happened. I called almost every important contact that I had been working with for the past three and a half years—phone calls were made, telegrams were sent. I chose not to take it lying down.

It would have been easy for Kessler to quasi-lick her wounds and just disappear. She chose not to, along with the support of friends and colleagues. Kessler chose not to have her public humiliation, and failure not to be tuned into the changing of the political winds, take her down.

Three Strikes and Not Out . . . Yet

Mark Goldston is desperately seeking a comeback. If you have seen a kid with lighted sneakers, thank Goldston—he's the co-inventor of them and a one-time president of L.A. Gear. Prior to L.A. Gear (now bankrupt), he was head of marketing at Reebok, where his moniker is on the inflatable "pump" sneaker. He's also been president of the Einstein Noah Bagel chain of restaurants—a financial fiasco.

Goldston's most recent endeavor is Netzero; most thought that he was taking on a dot-com mission impossible. Why? Because the company depended on banner ads that run all the time and it offered free Internet access to anyone who was willing to stand the ad barrage. The negative hook was that the longer someone was logged on, Netzero lost money. In the dot-com shake out of 2000, losing money wasn't a winning model.

As 2001 unfolded, so did the "free" ISP providers. Netzero's stock plummeted from a high of $40 a share in 2000 to below $1 in 2001. The most recent news is the company still has Goldston as the CEO, whether it survives or not, only time will tell. Although entrepreneur Goldston has had his business cosmic gooses, I suspect that he is desperately seeking a golden egg or two! He's still trying!

Finally, Getting Her Act Together

Oklahoma Personnel agency owner Jean Kelley has never done anything in a small way. In a two-year period, she was fired from six jobs.

> I have been in the personnel agency industry since 1969. Prior to that, I had held eight jobs in two years, of which I was fired from six of them. I was going to school at the same time and carried a 1.8 average in college. I ended up dropping out of that, too. By the time I was twenty-three, I was manager of the largest employment agency in Tulsa, Oklahoma. For the next three years, I maintained the highest sales record in the company as well as serving as its manager.

> When I was twenty-six, I opened Jean Kelley's Personnel with $7,200 borrowed from an uncle. My agreement with him was that he would finance my business and he would be my partner until I could give him a 100 percent return on his money. I was

very young and naive and I thought a 100 percent return on his money was a good deal for me. I later learned that it was because I couldn't have gotten the money from anywhere else. I had no serious collateral. Just myself and my work background.

When the recession hit in 1982, Tulsa was severely affected. We didn't have a recession, we had a depression. We were dependent on oil. My personal income dropped from $120,000 to $25,000 within twelve months. Now, a lot of people think that $25,000 is a lot of money, but I had expenses that matched $100,000 plus per year. I thought it was my fault. I could not buy the idea that there was this recession/depression going on.

As a salesperson, I am trained to think that you can do anything that you want to do and it's your fault if you don't do it. It was very hard for me to accept that any kind of outside circumstances— including the slashing of oil prices—would affect my income.

I went from a company of eight employees to two, which included myself. We moved from a spectacular suite of offices that overlooked the skyline of downtown Tulsa to cramped quarters that were no bigger than a closet. It was like starting all over again, but I didn't have my uncle's $7,200.

In addition to that I married in 1980, my first— being supermom with two step kids and I had cut my work down to forty-five hours a week. I was able to get up early, run three miles a day, begin to prepare supper, and by the time I got home from work at six, I could fix everything. It looked like we had the ideal family. The following year, I had to cope with this enormous personal/professional failure. My business. I was about to go out of business.

Most of the pain I felt was silent, most of the people I knew didn't know I was hurting so much. Philosophically, I had ingrained in me that you don't show other people your pain. That they don't care; after all, they have their own pain. So, here I was, an entrepreneur, alone and facing things like mortgaging the house to the max.

Kelley promised herself that she would never let her business interfere with her family, that she would never jeopardize their home with her business. To do that, she was faced with quite a few decisions. She reports that her husband was supportive during this time, and the whole situation was just quite bleak. Although several years have passed and she's doing quite well in business, she still has psychological scars. "It is really easy for me to get close to that pain. All I have to do is think about that time—it is still that fresh."

Keeper #10
Success usually comes through
the baptism of fire.
If you are stretching yourself,
there will be failure and crises.
You are the victor if you look
at it as a school of life.

Surviving a Firing

There are all levels of failure and crises. When one hits, it often becomes a significant motivating factor to make you do something—reevaluate, learn something new, and move forward. Men and women in our study said that after they had gone through a crisis, they felt initially weak—weak in the work force as well as who they were. But in the long run, they were much stronger and something positive was created.

Executive coach Patricia Goss remembers the time when she taught at City University in New York and was involved with the Faculty Senate. It was considering adding another foreign language to graduation requirements.

At City University, half of the students enrolled could not even speak English properly, much less adding a second foreign language. It was ludicrous. If anything, we should have required English as the first foreign language.

I stood up in the Faculty Senate and said, 'If you want to save each other's jobs, then let's figure out a way to save jobs. But let's not assume that we are going to save jobs in Romance languages or in Italian or in Greek by adding another language requirement. In the end, what we are going to do is upset the overall enrollment at the University. There will be confusion and people just won't come.

Being non-tenured, I was up for reappointment. That following Saturday, I got a letter in the mail that simply said that I was fired. I was stunned. I went back and traced through how I could have been fired.

Within my own department, it was unanimous to rehire me for a four-year reappointment. People in my department all had voted for me and thought it was outrageous that I had been fired. So they viewed me as on my way out and started to give me reasons why this could have happened. Everybody talked about it. And me.

I discovered that within the division of humanities, the negative votes came. The professors who taught Greek and Italian voted against me because of what I had said in the Faculty Senate meeting.

I had been fired for saying what I believed. I was absolutely shattered by it. It was a horrible feeling— total rejection. Not only was it a shock to me, but also I felt like my whole professional career was going down the drain. Within that period, I felt totally devalued as a person. I know that others had to feel that way, too.

And then, you begin to rethink what you did. I was such a fool to speak out the way I did, certainly without tenure. I kept saying to myself, "How could I have spoken my mind so freely without tenure?" I really began to beat myself up.

I was married to my first husband at the time, an attorney. He was furious. In fact, he was more upset than I was. Between him and a close friend, they carried more anger than I did. And with their anger, they pushed and encouraged me to fight it.

My husband wrote a nasty letter to the president of the university. My firing was overturned in very short order, but I never forgave them nor have I forgotten the fury of those many years ago.

No one believed it would be overturned. The consensus was that nothing would ever get changed to the right way once it has been wrong. When I won, everyone just sort of backed off and left me alone.

My husband felt it was a clear case of discrimination, of abridging my freedom of speech. But how many of us would have known that? More than likely, if I hadn't been married to him or a man like him, I would have been riddled with self-doubt, the university would have had its way, and I would have been left out in the cold.

Ironically, several years later, the women of City University won a multi-million dollar lawsuit for the type of thing that Goss went through.

An Affair to Delete

Before Bill Clinton's White House shenanigans were exposed with Monica Lewinsky, his head of HUD, Henry Cisneros, had his own run in with an extramarital affair. A major scandal at that time broke out with his cover up of the affair; his payoff to his mistress and a $10,000 fine for lying to the FBI. He was forced to resign from the Administration, a blow for Latinos who viewed Cisneros position with great pride.

In a recent interview with Helen Thorpe, Cisneros said, "It's been a relief for put it at rest legally, but it's never behind one emotionally, intellectually, because it was so painful and so much a part of my life for so long." He adds,

I'm sobered by it, and humbled, and constantly ask for the spiritual strength to march forward as optimistically about life as I can.

I learned a lot from the man who was my boss, Bill Clinton, about how you get up every day and see the world fresh and just keep going, not matter what. When I was really down on myself, he just wouldn't hear of quitting. He said, 'Of course not. Do your job. Just keep going.'

Cisneros went on to say that he has dealt with the past, so be it; that his family is well and that he has had much success in business since his resignation. His experience could have left him feeling that he was a victim; that the media and political enemies had done him in. He chose not to go down that path. On his last day as President, Bill Clinton granted Cisneros a pardon.

Any of these men and women could have thrown in the towel. But didn't. Their experiences, their failures, their survivals, are all a testament to their ability, a learned ability that allows them to take in the big picture.

When crisis hits, whatever the crisis is, step back. Take a breath, probably several. Call a trusted friend, your spouse or partner in life, someone who cares about you. Values you. And is nonjudgmental. You may need some help bringing the situation into perspective—to grasp what really is going on.

Every failure, every crisis, can become an enormous opportunity. The word for crisis in Chinese consists of two characters—one for danger and one for opportunity.

So, for every dangerous situation, there is an opportunity that can be learned from-where you can grow from and reach out and develop yourself further. None of us likes to experience the crises of life, the failures that we encounter. It does help, though, to take a little bit of the sting out of the impact to know that, without question, growth will come from it.

Keeper #11
Any failure that you are, or have experienced,
passes. It will become yesterday's.
Not today's. Not tomorrow's. The decision
on how to handle it is something that
you control. Only you.

The definition of failure is not the act of failure, whatever the failure is. The definition of failure is when you don't get up and try again. The phoenix does rise. Again. And again.

Chapter Eight

Step #7

Expect the Unexpected . . . It's Life

Life is like a ferris wheel. Sometimes you're up, and sometimes you're down. But, it's always moving.

Sarah Weddington
A Matter of Choice

Confident men and women have learned to look at themselves. There have been many times when they have had to step back and take a snapshot of what was going on and what the situation was that they were in. At the same time, they reached out to trusted friends and colleagues to get feedback for the pickle they found themselves in. You'll find that you will to.

The Worst Wasn't Expected

The worst day of professor, lawyer, author and women's activist Sarah Weddington's life was when President Jimmy Carter went down in defeat in his bid for re-election in 1980. One day she was a critical and major advisor to the President of the United States, the next, nothing. After the people spoke from their voting booths, she was fired, plain and simple. Her president was out . . . and so was she. Sarah shares,

> When the voters spoke in the Carter-Reagan election, they set off tsunami waves in Washington DC in one day. I went from being Assistant to the President of the United States with an office just above the Oval Office and access to the most powerful levers to create change in the world—to having two months to move out.
>
> Almost everyone I knew, including me, lost their jobs that day. One couldn't call friends to ask their help in relocating. They were all looking too!
>
> But moving out forced me to reassess my skills and how I wanted to spend my time. It resulted in a new career as a writer, a speaker and a teacher. I'm less stressed and happier now, but I am so glad that I had that priceless chance which so few have to experience American life from the top.

The media reported that the election was close. Even though it was close, each side always assumes that they will be the victor—it's one of the great things that drives the political scene. Sarah Weddington didn't believe that

Jimmy Carter would be defeated. He was. She hadn't expected the unexpected.

The Unexpected Leads to Being the First

Next up at the Reagan election plate was Walter Mondale. In 1984, he did the unexpected and selected Congresswoman Geraldine Ferraro as the first woman to be nominated for vice president of the United States by a major political party. Although the Mondale-Ferraro team lost the election, Ferraro has surfaced not only a survivor, but also a winner.

During the election, she hadn't expected that the media would focus on the activities of her husband or son . . . or that they would become "game" for their attentions. She had expected that the media would concentrate on her track record as a U.S. Congresswoman. Wrong assumption.

Since 1984, she has been constantly in the public eye. Not all of it has been fun, as she said in an interview in *USA Today:*

> If I look back on the whole thing, I think it was very positive. It took down once and for all the exclusion of women from national politics. When Representative Pat Schroeder withdrew from the race for nominee for president, no one giggled that a woman can't do it. In 1984, Fritz Mondale removed the final barrier from women achieving political power.
>
> Nineteen eighty-four was an incredible opportunity for me. It doesn't leave one bitter about the outcome or how my family was treated during the

campaign. I genuinely feel my husband and my son were singled out. That doesn't make us bitter. Being bitter can cause you real problems. I'm not going to let that happen to me. I figured out very young in life you make the best of your circumstances. How can you feel bitter?

Home on the Range

Wayne Hage is a rancher; entrepreneur, married and the father of two daughters. He owns 7000 acres spread over 11 square miles in Idaho. Hage's book, *Stewards of the Range*, exposes the problems private ranchers have had with the Federal Government in what are called "takings" cases. Cases where the feds declare private property public, or at least under the control of the Government. The private landowner is pushed aside, more times than not, paid far less than the land is worth. The Idaho organization, Stewards of the Range, was created in 1992, taking its name from the painting by cowboy artist J. N. Swanson.

He said, "Either you have the right to own property or you are property." He has spent the past two decades fighting the U.S. Forest Service with a case valued at approximately $28 million. The Forest Service wants the water, land and cattle grazing rights. His ranch. His life. With over 20 court hearings behind him, he and his daughter Margaret Gabbard, the executive director of Stewards of the Range shared,

The Forest Service objective is to scare us and run us off our ranch. We are a patriotic family, loving the principles of what our country was based on. We've worked hard all our lives to build and maintain the beautiful spread that we have.

To date, we've been in court over 20 times, each time winning. In 1992, we hit a low spot. The Forest Service made false accusations publicly lying in court that I was cutting down and selling valuable timber on our property. I was convicted of a felony. Within a short period of time, the 9th Circuit Court reversed the conviction, for all I had done was remove a small tree from a ditch. On the ranch, it's know as maintenance.

We've learned through our experiences with the Government that too much power can lead anyone astray. At this point, we have little respect for the Government.

Hage's run in with the Forest Service was certainly unexpected. His work and positioning has taken courage to continue the long drawn-out fight. His position, "When the Government owns 51% of the property, it no longer has to come to us," is ingrained in his continued fight not to cave in to the unrelenting onslaught to intimidate him, his family and their integrity.

Renegotiating Your Goals

Sometimes you have unrealistic expectations for yourself. You find out that perhaps you cannot attain something at this very moment . . . you need to learn that that's fine, it doesn't mean that if you can't get it now, it's a failure. It means it is just not our time. You need to re-negotiate.

There are always options. One of the biggest revelations I've learned is that you have a choice. And that choice often rears its head when an individual begins to assess what's happening, who they are and where they're going.

Choice ties into control. There are times when you can control a situation, much like a master puppeteer pulling strings, planning movements and events. But what happens when you can't control those strings that life sometimes tosses your way—those strings that seem to tie everything, including you, up in knots?

Choice enters the picture. Yours.

Previous research for my books *Woman to Woman 2000: Becoming Sabotage Savvy in the New Millennium* and *Woman to Woman: From Sabotage to Support* showed that women were more likely to try and "fix" something, whatever that something was—a bad relationship at home or work, a perceived injustice; that women were more likely to spend negative energy/thinking on getting back at someone if they had betrayed them personally or professionally; that women tended to personalize issues, places, and things and when they did, they reacted personally—they felt hurt, pained, betrayed. My research also found that reactions, even immediate assessments, often were blown out of proportion as to what really happened.

Men didn't focus on fixing things or stuff; they didn't want to put energy into anything that was a one way street or a no return for them; and they didn't feel personally betrayed, because the simple fact was that they would put themselves in a position where personal information was revealed that could backfire on them.

It is important to keep in mind that you choose your

friends, whom you play with, where you apply for a job, and usually where you go to school. You can't choose the family that you are born into but you can choose "second" families or "heart" families, as I call them. You may not have a terrific family that nourishes you, supports you. Many don't. We found that it was not uncommon to get their support from others if it was not at "home." Some said that they adopted new families.

Family, friends, and certain colleagues—these are the people, the groups, who are there for you—there for you in stepping back and helping you assess your situation. Listen to their input. Does it sound right, deep down? That small voice in your belly can lead to quite a roar. A roar that is, when you choose not to listen to it.

There will be many times when you want to throw in the towel; that, again, is your choice. Before you do, though, assess the situation, and seek input from a trusted adviser and/or friend.

Many people are very organized and methodical about their work, which definitely carries over into their personal lives. To them, I say, nothing comes overnight and nothing comes without work. You can't snap your fingers and have it. Everything comes gradually. Don't set goals that at the moment may be unrealistic.

Unexpected Sales Creates Billions

One of the most successful Internet companies—in increased shareholder value and one that actually makes a profit—is eBay. Its CEO is Meg Whitman. Whitman's strengths are that she is incredibly flexible and can adapt to multiple opportunities. Her guidance has revolutionized the Internet flea market of resales.

Coming from the old school of corporate life—with time at Procter & Gamble, Disney, Hasbro, and FTD—she served as a brand manager to a CEO. At no point was she recognized as a star, or even potential star. Jumping to eBay made her a billionaire. And a Star. Not bad for someone who values the time she had along with her career to raise her kids.

In her position, it's not uncommon for the unexpected to surface. A clue to someone's strength is how she or he responds to the unexpected. In 1999, Whitman shined. The eBay site crashed numerous times, one lasting as long as 22 hours. As she said,

I missed that one.

Whitman blamed herself for not making sure the infrastructure of eBay was as strong as it needed to be. Her remedy was to dig in and learn everything that she could about what made eBay tick. Crashes in the future aren't welcomed. Prior to eBay, most people bought stuff from stores, catalogs, the flea market, auctions or a garage sale. Prior to eBay, most people sold stuff via an auction, flea market or garage sale. Unless you were a retailer, you didn't sell through a store or catalog. eBay introduced a seller, any seller to a million plus potential buyers. The new way for the new Millennium.

You Can't Please Them All

As I write this chapter, I'm somewhere between Honolulu and San Francisco. I've just come from a presentation I did at the annual convention for a national association. We had a great time; at least I think most of us did. The preceding night at the closing gala, several of the men and women at the table I sat at said that they heard they missed a terrific program—mine. A speaker loves to hear that kind of buzz, but did everyone feel that way? Most likely, no.

I have a routine ritual I do after an event. When the program host obtains evaluations, I go through them after everyone is gone. I read every comment. Some said I had a great sense of humor, that I was magnificent and terrific, loved my outfit, that they laughed all the way through the program, and that they wanted more time with me. And then, ten evaluations later, I read, "Disorganized, this person is tight, needs to have more humor, a waste of time, earrings too big!" I found a few other instances in which participants totally and completely had a 180-degree different opinion about me.

One raving and glowing about exactly the same thing that somebody else rated me deficient. What gives? I know that I'm a good speaker and that I have a sense of humor (although truth be told, it is sometimes quirky). Here's how I look at it. I want/expect everyone in my audiences to have a good time, come away with some solid information that they can implement in their personal and professional lives and feel they want more. That's what I expect.

In reality, I know that there will be some people that I just don't fully connect with—the wrong fit. The unexpected. That evening at the gala, my husband and I thought the entertainer was fantastic—another couple at our table rarely laughed like we did and they left early. I expected and had a great time, and I think they didn't. I got what I expected—they, most likely, didn't . . . the unexpected. With what I experienced, I felt/expected everyone there to think he was terrific too. Obviously, I was wrong.

You can drive yourself nuts by letting other people's opinions really determine how you think about yourself. The important thing is to really do the best that you can and ask yourself are you putting yourself out there 100 percent plus most of the time and not taking all the negative feedback so personally. Not everyone is going to love you 100 percent of the time. That's the bottom line in the speaking business. Thankfully, they're in the minority.

When Karen Kessler of the Mondale campaign was unceremoniously told on national television that she was fired, she certainly didn't expect to hear it. Her thoughts,

> When I got back to the hotel room, I was able to sit down and assess what was going on. Would Walter Mondale want to fire me or was it directed from some other source? How committed was I to the organization? And, then, I put together a plan. I assessed what I thought had happened, learned what did happen, and then was able to move on.

Create a Gratitude List

Personnel agency owner Jean Kelley feels it is important to make a gratitude list.

> When you are in the middle of a situation that is not going well, in fact, it can be a downright disaster, it's important to have a list that you can go to and can

acknowledge. Every day I make out a list of my assets as well as a gratitude list, a list that lets me know what I am thankful for—my sight, my hands, my feet, my house, my home, even my car.

Many people who feel as if they are down on their luck still have transportation to drive—think about the millions of people who will never even get in a car. Those who are down on their luck usually have a roof over their heads and a car to drive. They may be floating around on pity. It's important to sit down and really assess what is going on in your life, to do a reality check. Most of us can move on from the *woe-is-me* to *life-is-not-so-bad*.

Businesswoman Lucy Hillestad also feels it is important to make a list, she calls it the "what is best about me" list.

What is best about me—is it my eyes, my hair, do I have nice nails, can I type, can I talk, can I listen, can I learn, am I a good manager, do I know how to lead, am I creative, etc.? Whatever those things are, use them to your best advantage. Whether you are at the fourth-grade level or the Ph.D. level, it is always the same; use the tools you have if you want to move on.

Think about it, no matter what it is. You have to assess and reassess where you are as well as what's happening around you. If you like yourself, someone else is going to like you. If you don't, no one is going to like you so you better begin with yourself. Look in the mirror and start discovering what is it about you that other people could like? What do these people see?

Start building on that one thing and day-by-day as you look in the mirror, especially when bad things happen in our lives, there is always something good that will come back at you. My mother used to say to me, "Maybe today wasn't such a good day, but tomorrow the sun is going to come up and there's going to be a silver lining in the clouds." And I believed her. I can almost hear her say it now even though she has been dead for several years.

Keeper #12
If you believe that all goes as planned,
you're living in a tunnel with blindfolds on.
By expecting the unexpected, you stay
at the top of your game. Good for you, and
good for those you work and live with.

Time Makes the Difference

Whenever anything happens unexpectedly, it's common to expect a correction almost immediately. You may think that surely they will know that there is a mistake; that anything negative that has happened will turn positive very soon. Not always. Author Carole Hyatt feels that it's important to give yourself time; that rarely do things happen or change overnight.

It's important to give yourself some time, a space for time for only you. Allow yourself the time to see what's actually happened. You may think that you can't afford it, but you'll need it. Not an indefinite time, but a time to get through. It's like when your confidence has been shattered, it's like an open wound—all wounds need to heal. And each of us has a different timetable—some need a weekend, some need six months. By giving yourself time to sit back and look at what happened and assess the situation, your confidence can be rebuilt. After all, you deserve it.

Sometimes when your confidence is at a low ebb, you feel generally miserable. Your work product deteriorates. Dr. Deborah Bright is the author of several best selling books including *On the Edge and in Control* and *Gearing Up for the Fast Lane.* Heading a consulting firm in New York, she does nationwide programs for clients that include IBM, the FBI, and the Detroit Tigers. Her experience as an Olympic diver influences her work today.

I think sports are like business. You're always having to prove yourself, you can't rest on your past successes in sports. After a particularly lousy workout, when I was diving, I was so upset I can still remember my coach's words: "Listen, Deb, you have everything that it takes to be a champion, everything. All you have to do is believe in yourself and be confident and you have it."

I was very young then, in my mid-teens, and winning everything in the state of Florida. After being ranked number one on the East Coast, I had to make a tough decision. Should I remain the big fish in a small pond or should I move on and possibly risk being the small fish in a big pond? I wanted to go to the next bigger pond and I always did. I always said that I would rather not be the big fish in the small pond; I am going to shoot to be the little fish in the big pond.

When she told me that I had everything it takes to be a champion, in combination with my desire to be at the Olympics, I decided to take the risk, shooting to be the little fish in the big pond. All I could think about was being an Olympic champion. My coach was the former national champion. It means a lot to you when somebody says that I could be the best.

During this workout, I couldn't do anything right, every dive I tried, I landed over or I would land short. It became impossible for me to land in the water vertically. I couldn't get the momentum up to do the twist. I couldn't get my hips up. Everything was going against me. I felt like such a klutz. My self-doubt grew bigger and bigger. How was I ever going to go out and compete and achieve any of my goals? I tried to hold back the tears. I started to cry.

What she said to me was that she believed in me. It was very powerful and it dawned on me, you just have to have confidence, it is so easy to say it, but how do you put it 'into practice? To me, crisis and the like are just an aspect of living, it's not an exception, it's just an aspect. It would be nice if it didn't happen, but there are no guarantees and life was never promised as being 100 percent wonderful.

Again, I thought about what my coach had said earlier. I got goose bumps. 'Somebody believes in me,' I said to myself, and at the same time a lump formed in my throat.

Survival and Thrival

Consultant and corporate trainer Leslie Charles was able to find her confidence when she went on welfare, went back to school to get educated, broke out and started on her own, eventually even taking a new name. There was a period of time after her divorce when things started to go well. Then Charles hit several bumps. Her son was killed, her horse died, and she suffered a health crisis. She felt that she was on a downhill spiral—every time she would pick herself up, something else hit. The unexpected.

My son died in 1984. 1 did a lot of my grief therapy on the back of my horse. I had been a horse owner since I was twenty-nine, even when I was on welfare. I gave up all alcohol and cigarettes so I could ride. I had a friend who kept him for $20 a month and I figured if I gave up smoking and drinking, I could afford to keep my horse.

When my horse died in 1987, it brought back a lot of my son's death. I have been through enough to know that to regain my confidence, I had to do it internally. Today, I do a workshop on personal power and tie in confidence. I came to my definition of confidence by starting in the dictionary. I looked up 'power.' The dictionary says that power is the capacity to do or to act, so it's internal. I therefore view personal power and confidence as one and the same.

Personal power is confidence and confidence is

personal power. It's so easy to regress. I like to look at building confidence and regaining it after each of these crises that I've gone through in small steps. Forget the big steps. I think you have to move in a gradual upward trend, but allow yourself to go through a comfort zone.

As I move along, the more I stretch my comfort zone, the more comfortable I become with being uncomfortable. In the old days, when I felt uncomfortable, I would literally stop in my tracks. I wouldn't do it anymore, whatever it was that was making me uncomfortable. In fact, sometimes I withdrew.

Leslie Charles has survived, and thrived, through a number of unexpected events—all events that became cosmic gooses that moved her to another level. With survival and thrival, she's developed a set of tools that she can tap into if the unexpected lands on her doorstep.

Pass the Cake!

Management consultant Nicole Schapiro has experienced more than her share of personal crises and unexpected events. And the depths of her personal crises are far greater than most of us will ever know. Nicole Schapiro was a Hungarian refugee. Throughout Schapiro's journey for survival, she has learned that the territory of the workplace is really no different from the territory of life.

Several times, she has had to choose to survive or to give up. She has each time assessed the skills that she had in order to learn to see things that others really can't see. She can remember her fifteenth birthday only too well. The time—the Hungarian Revolution. It was a small group of comrades. An onion was the only food. She asked each one of them to imagine and visualize that onion as a birthday cake—dark chocolate decorated with purple flowers. It was something that she needed to believe in, that it would be a celebration acknowledging her life as a person. She remembers the wise words from her grandfather—her Poppa, "Confidence comes from remembering all the things that Poppa used to say. That with positive thinking, you can truly overcome anything negative."

Assess Yourself

When I am trying to assess a situation now, I go away for a weekend. I go someplace that I can really enjoy, not someplace I might miss being with my spouse, not someplace that I would miss friendships—someplace that gives me a lot of joy. For some, it's the beach, others a spa. If you like the beach, go to a wonderful beach. If you enjoy fitness, go to a spa, but don't engage in all the social activities there.

Do things that make you feel good, exercise, sitting on the beach, watching the waves or skiing all day, but the key is to spend the day with yourself. Take along a pen and pencil and write down your pro and con columns. Where are you in your life? What is good? What is bad? Where had you hoped to be in your life at this point? Which of these things are fantasy and which of these things are realistically obtainable? Then, come out with a formula of where you would like to be next year at this time and then create a plan on how to get it.

> *Keeper #13*
> *If you will combine the knowledge, success,*
> *and control of previous experiences and*
> *then apply them to future situations,*
> *your confidence is guaranteed to grow.*
> *That growth comes from assessing*
> *where you are as you gain control and/or*
> *perspective of unexpected events.*

All of us will have unexpected events. Dorothy had it when she landed in the land of the Munchkins and felt totally alone. As she met up with the tin man, the scarecrow and the cowardly lion, each was unexpected. Harry Potter encountered unexpected event after unexpected event at Hogwarts. When his uncle finally moved him out from under the stairway in the "family" home, it was the totally unexpected. Who would have thought that messages and mail would be carried by owls and not the mailman? Certainly not Harry Potter!

The bottom line is that you will encounter a myriad of unexpected events. Some will be quite pleasant. Others, a major disaster. When that happens, it's normal to feel alone, afraid, even without worth. It's the recognition of what's happening, the ability to evaluate and acknowledge where you are, and, finally, the belief that you can move forward. With confidence.

Chapter Nine

Step #8

Create Bravos . . . Take Your Credit

No one can make you feel inferior without your permission.

Eleanor Roosevelt

When you are in the depths of despair; when you think that you are facing the biggest problem that you have ever looked at; if you are immersed in a major disaster or have just exited one, you may have thought or are thinking that you are worthless. You may think that nothing you did was right or that there was no solution to the situation. Sound familiar? Are you feeling that way now? You are not alone. Thousands, even millions, have walked in your shoes—have felt exactly as you feel.

The men and women in our survey reported that

they didn't always take credit for their accomplishments. Women and men were fairly equal when they said that they *always* did (8% versus 10% of men); *often,* women did 47% versus 53% of men; and 3% of the women, 5% of the men said that they *rarely* took credit. The big difference occurred in the *sometimes* category. For women, 42% said that they *sometimes* took credit versus 32% of the men.

Collectively, 45% of the women and 37% of the men said that they sometimes or rarely took credit for accomplishments. This has bad news, and good news to it. The bad news is that too, too many don't pat themselves on the back. The good news is that the more successful you are, or want to be; the more you take credit for what you do. Openly and without reservation.

The Lid Lady Doesn't Count

Several years ago, I was referred to an organization to speak at their annual meeting. This was a group that I thought my skills and topics would be a perfect fit for. Just prior to a week of other speaking engagements, I spoke with the woman who would select speakers, sending her a press kit, copies of several of my books, audio and videotapes.

The morning I was back in my office, a call came from her. Just sharing with my staff what a great week I had and how terrific the audiences and groups that I worked with were, I took her call. I was in a grand mood . . . but not for long. Within minutes, she proceeded to tell me that she didn't like the way I looked, walked, interacted, and dressed. She told me that I was totally disorganized, had no sense of humor and couldn't tell a story. Then, she told me I needed to go back to school to learn how to write!

A few moments ago, I felt great. I now felt like garbage and a little stunned with her feedback. Finally saying to her, "I guess we won't be working together," she agreed, and hung up on me! Major bummer—and a tad depressing.

During this time, one of my daughters worked for me. When I hung up the phone, she simply asked, "Who was that?" I told her.

Sheryl went over to one of our files and pulled one out. She said, "Mom, here is a letter from Tom Peters, Barbara Bush, Ann Richards, Diane Sawyer, Jane Pauley and Jack Canfield. Mom, this woman does not count."

Does not count? Of course, Sheryl was right. But still, that woman said all those things about me.

That night, several of my friends were over for dinner. I told them what had happened earlier in the day. One of them got up from the table and went into my kitchen. We heard cupboard doors opening. She returned with a large green trash bag and said, "Where are they?" The "they" was the product of the company— a product that most kitchens have somewhere tucked away in a cupboard, usually separated from the lids they originally came with.

That night, six of us created an exorcism—all of the "product", every piece that I had, departed from my home, never to be welcomed again. I was an excellent speaker, and am. I do have a sense of humor and love to tell stories. For whatever reason, this woman and I did not click.

A few years later, I was speaking for a group in

Florida and shared this story. One of the participants approached me later and said, "I know who you are talking about. It's _____". She was right and affirmed that I wasn't alone—she used to work with her!

Keeper #14
Do not take a NO from someone who doesn't have the authority or power to say yes. Don't waste your time.

The Electronic Elephant

GE's Jack Welch was a tad slow on embracing the Internet. From zero personal use of email before 1999 (even gloating in 1996 at a *FORTUNE* 500 CEO Forum that he didn't have a computer in his own office and didn't need one), he's now an evangelist on how the Internet has been integrated to GE's overall business strategy. Once his foot, or computer, was in the door, team GE did things differently.

Sun Microsystems' CEO, Scott McNealy and Welch get together at least once a year for the annual Welch Cup—a golf tournament between the two legendary CEOs that was fostered by McNealy. McNealy refers to Welch, and GE, as the Internet grizzly. In his analogy, the Internet grizzly is charging down the path. Noting that it would be helpful if you have some decent shoes on in an attempt to outrun the grizzly, you stop to put on a pair of running shoes so you can go faster. McNealy's point being that you don't have to outrun everybody—the grizzlies—all you have to do is outrun your competitors. Which is what GE does—it's the elephant, but the fastest one going.

Welch, at this writing, is in his 70th year. He plans on retiring within the year. He will tell you, when asked the question, is GE ahead of the game, even or way behind?—that his company, via his vision and decades of action, is way ahead of their competitive field; if looked at as a standard in business, way behind. All in all, if Welch had not had grasped the value of the Internet, GE would still be an elephant, but most likely, a gasping one. His wake-up to what the Internet was and could do for his company (and himself) became the cosmic goose to get going. The golden egg is multiplying every day.

Write It Down

Many of our respondents who did take credit for their accomplishments said they liked to make lists of things that they are proud of. Lists that make them feel good. Lists that help keep them in the world of reality. These lists even keep them in balance.

Personnel agency owner Jean Kelley is a list maker.

Make a list of your assets and read them every single morning. If you can't think of anything good about yourself, when you are in a downward spiral or bad situation, make a list of everything that anyone ever said about you since you were one year old. If you have pretty hair, a nice smile, a great personality, if you're good at math, if you made a walkie-talkie when you were a little kid, if you were one of the best skateboarders in the neighborhood, if you could jump rope faster than anyone, if you made the best chocolate chip cookies around, if you wrap the most unusual presents, whatever it is, write down what someone made a fuss over.

What Kelley is really recommending is very similar to taking out a piece of paper—my favorite is a yellow legal pad—and writing in all the "pros" about you. Label the top "Terrific Things I Did" and start writing them down: what's happened at work, what kind of comments people have made about past jobs that you were involved in; kudos from your network group; referrals you have given that have landed someone a job; a promotion; giving credit to someone; making someone look terrific.

Think about your family—describe some of the fun times you've had when you've gotten together; times you've been silly, times when you share and care; times when you allow yourself to be you. And surround yourself with people who make you feel special, who accept you with all your blemishes—even warts!

Create a Measurement

Successful people usually look at how far they have come. They aren't famished for attention or recognition. That doesn't mean that they don't have big ambitions. A common attitude was that if you are going to fail, you might as well fail having a big goal, a big dream.

Establishing external recognition from others of your work and your capabilities becomes a critical factor in your check-up. Look back at periods when you felt depressed or low. During that time, you probably felt invisible—you weren't recognized or appreciated for who or what you've done. From others, or from yourself. Recognition and appreciation needs to come from yourself as well as others.

So, if you are in the cycle of non-recognition of what you do—and have done—from yourself and others, what can you do to break out of the cycle? Try the simple technique of getting out a legal pad and writing down all the terrific things that you've done in the past. It may ease whatever personal agony you may be in and allow you to get things back into perspective. In that process, it's amazing that solutions seem to float out for just about anything. Your accomplishments from the past actually trigger ideas to help solve a current dilemma, whatever it may be.

Keeper #15
Everyone has a bum day, time or event.
You are not alone nor specifically selected
when things go wrong. It happens.
This is the time to be your own friend—
celebrate and cheer the things that
you have done, and will do.

When I speak to groups on *The Confidence Factor* and the research behind it, I often ask for a volunteer who has had a bum week, month, even year, from the audience before the program. I assure them what all she or he has to do is minimal: I will ask their name, what they do, and then I will make up a story about them. I tell them I want to make them feel better. And believe it or not, it happens in less than a minute!

When I get to the Create Bravos segment of my program, I call my "volunteer" forth by name, bringing them to the stage. After being introduced to the audience, I share my "made-up" story about what they do. In it, everything is rather grandiose—the theme identifies them as the best this or the best that. The audience is then asked to stand up. I tell them that if they have the whistling gift, be prepared to whistle; I ask the audience to bravo, to applaud, to hoot, to do whatever they do when they are feeling great about someone or a presentation they have just heard. The noise can be thundering.

My volunteer just stands there. The audience does the rest. I tell the audience the story of the amazing, remarkable thing that this woman or man has done that nobody knew about, that no one gave them credit for or acknowledged. Then, we applaud, hoot and hollar for them for fifteen to thirty seconds depending on when I cut it off. The volunteer gets the standing ovation of a lifetime that few ever receive.

Do they feel silly? Oh, sometimes, and they say, "I feel a little silly." But then when I ask them, "Do you feel better?" Their response, "Yes. I absolutely feel better." I've had women and men bow, curtsy, even ask the audience to give them more! I had one woman break down in tears. It's amazing how good we can feel when we get credit for our accomplishments—from others . . . and ourselves. And, in only a minuscule amount of time.

> ### Keeper #16
> *If you don't take credit for your accomplishments, whatever they may be, however big or small . . . someone else will. It's not fair; it's not ethical; but it's life.*

Women are more likely than men to have grown up under the umbrella that it's not nice to brag. Scrap the old messages and practices. If you don't pat yourself on the back, who well? Your competitors? Your boss? Your spouse or partner? How about the kids? Your friends? Most of us assume that others know when and that they've done something good or terrific. Here's the simple truth: they don't. You get to tell them, and yourself.

Do so by creating a nice letter or pats on the back file—you may be the only correspondent in it, that doesn't matter. When someone dings you or things aren't going as smoothly as you'd like, you can dig in and review times when all was well. Who did you surround yourself with? What were you doing? Can any of that be recreated to get you back on track?

I have made it a practice to keep the cards and letters I get. Some are from readers of my books; some are from audience participants and meeting planners; some are from friends and family. At times, they have been an inspiration, at others, a mirror to probe. At all times, they are golden eggs.

Chapter Ten

Step #9

Keep in Circulation . . . Visibility Counts

When your life is crushed, you have to have a good support network around you. You can't disappear.
Terry Neese, Founder-Grass Roots Impact
owner-Terry Neese Personnel Services

It is not uncommon to create distance when the chips are down. The most common response is to step out the limelight and create distance. Distance from strangers. Distance from friends. Even distance from yourself. Survey respondents said that they *often* withdrew from others when things went wrong (72% women and 63% men); 28% of the women and 37% of the men said that they *rarely* withdrew themselves. The overwhelming majority said they "want to be alone." An accompanying attitude was that others would recognize the good that they did (it didn't matter if it was a workplace or personal issue) and what they had accomplished on their merits alone.

Do not—hear me—do not take this attitude. It's the kiss of death. Yours. When confidence-shattering situations erupt, THIS is the time to stand out. You are being watched. Casually and microscopically. People are ready to dissect you—all the good, all the bad, and definitely, all the ugly.

It's wise to not wallow in self-pity. You will be amazed at how others will come forward and pat you on the back. Pats on the back help to regain a fractured confidence. Part of getting back on your feet involves others—you reaching out to them. Granted, it's important to pat yourself of the back, but it's also imperative that you do something for someone else—reach out and find others to do things for. Keep in mind Abraham Lincoln's words, "People are as happy as they make up their minds to be."

Sometimes you have to force yourself to mend, to circulate—whether it's a meal appointment, sport date, some type of social engagement—it doesn't matter, the point is to stay in circulation.

Keeper #17
Being a hermit is not an option.
If you choose to remove yourself from
the mainstream, no one knows you're alive.

Power Plays

FORTUNE magazine named Terry Neese one of the top 30 power players on Capitol Hill in 2000. Her expertise— business, especially women business owners. Currently, Neese wears multiple hats. She's the owner of Terry Neese Personnel Services in Oklahoma City, OK, the co-founder of GrassRoots Impact, specializing in corporate and political strategy and a fierce advocate for small businesses. She's a past president of NAWBO—the National Association of Women Business Owners and has run for political office.

It's not uncommon for people to see business owners, especially those frequently cited in the media as having the good life. No problems, be happy everywhere. There has not been a business owner or leader that I have met that hasn't had a few confidence crushers along the way. Terry Neese is no exception.

In the early nineties, she decided that she needed to give back more to her community. Oklahoma's economy was in the doldrums from the oil bust of the eighties. She believed that the only way to bring back the economy was through the free enterprise system. In her opinion, that meant generating more small businesses. In her words,

I had never been political in my life and at the age of 40 (1990), I thought it was time for me to give back to the community and help the state grow. I though the best venue was the Lt. Governor's office because of its focus on economic development. So, with no political base or knowledge, I announced for Lt. Governor of Oklahoma. I began to speak across the state, picking up support. I was the only person in the race for months. The Republican Party leaders didn't know me. I'm sure they thought who in the world is this businesswoman? We must get some-one to run for this office who can win! So, they recruited a former state representative, minority leader and the current Secretary of Transportation. Well, almost everyone told me that I couldn't beat him. No Way!

I defeated him and became the first woman nomi-nated for Lt. Governor in the State of Oklahoma. In order to win, it got pretty nasty. The guy I defeated wouldn't endorse me and in fact worked against me. So, I lost the general election. I had NEVER LOST anything in my life! I was devastated and cried for weeks. My self-esteem was crushed. I couldn't go out in public. It was terrible. Never, did I stop to realize what I had accomplished. Never did I stoop and pat myself on the back and realize that I beat a well-known public figure. I didn't really lose. I WON! But, I didn't look at it that way, not then.

It took me a good year to pull myself up and once I did, I spent the next four years paying my dues in the Party. Working precincts, contributing to the party, fund raising. You name it, I did it. When 1994 rolled around, I announced that I would run again for Lt. Governor. I was the only one in the race for a long time and then a female state representative announced for Lt. Governor. I should have realized at the time that the "ole boys were going to teach me a lesson, because women are not supposed to defeat men."

So, they recruited this woman to go after me and she did. I raised huge amounts of money, and I had great grassroots support. But, five days before the election, she found a disgruntled former employee who had left the agency two to three years prior and had filed a frivolous lawsuit on me. I lost the election by less than 6,000 votes. The day after the election, the lawsuit was dropped. She went on to win the general elections. The first woman, the first Republican woman to win the Lt. Governor's office.

After the election was over, transition of the team in government began. The message was conveyed to me that I would never be anything in the Republican Party nor have any role in the state so long as she was the Lt. Governor.

This time, I WAS really devastated. I literally wanted to leave the state. Fortunately, the National Association of Women Business Owners needed a consultant with human resource and management skills for some "turn around" non-profit association restructuring. I moved to Washington D.C. and spent 24 hours a day rebuilding NAWBO's infrastructure, raising corporate dollars and building their public policy initiatives on Capitol Hill. I consulted for them for three years. During that time, I started my new consulting firm, GrassRoots Impact and turned Terry Neese Personnel Services over to my daughter to run.

For the past three years, I have been building my new company; I'm politically involved at the national level and work closely with many Congressmen and women. I'm making a difference in the lives of small business owners across the nation due to my advocacy on their behalf on Capitol Hill and now represent almost 350,000 small business owners when I testify before Congress or move legislation forward.

I believe I was just not supposed to be Lt. Governor of Oklahoma. I was pushing it to make it so; but that was not where I was supposed to be. I'm doing the work I love and the work God intended me to do. Besides, I think it is a higher calling!

When your life is crushed, you have to have a good support network around you. I had that with my husband and my daughter and my mother. You have to have the will power to move on, the confidence that you can endure and the strength to carry on.

Neese's personal story of dreams, defeat, sabotage, assessing, redirecting, reinventing herself, identifying her strengths and weaknesses, getting feedback from those she trusted and getting back out in circulation all wave the banner for confidence. She's got it, only strengthened by the setbacks of the political arena.

Your Circle, Your Life

So, whom do you hang out with? At work, at home, at play? For me, one thing was to keep myself surrounded with those that I wanted to see the most. People who made me feel good, not those who would dominate me. Not those who were always trying to change me or put me down. Rather, the people who would accept me for who I was.

Staying in circulation means that you're willing to be

responsible for yourself. I know when some people hear the word "responsible," they think, "Oh my God, I have to look at my faults. I have to see how I've screwed up this time."

That's not what being responsible is about. Responsible means looking at your life. Here are the things that have happened to you, now what do you want to do about them? What are you willing to do to make the changes? The more that you beat yourself up, the more no one is going to be willing to help you stop. You need to say, "Wait a minute, I spent a lot of time criticizing myself and it's not working. There's got to be something good about me. Where is it?" I am in this world for a reason and I'm willing to find out what I need to do.

Believe it or not, keeping in circulation is rather like self-preservation. Keeping in circulation weaves through all components to building confidence.

- When you are courageous and take care of yourself, you are more inclined to be out in the forefront where others can see you.

- When you don't bottle things up and talk to others and get feedback, your circulation movement will start off with a bang.

- When you work around others whom you admire and are positive, and you review your past accomplishments—those pats on the back— you are more than likely to move away from any past bitterness that you might feel.

- When you assess the situation that you've come through looking for both the strengths and weaknesses in unexpected events and make the decision to learn something new, you stretch yourself and force yourself out, making it almost impossible to be a hermit.

- When you finally understand that you are not alone and thousands have walked in the same shoes that you're wearing, feeling the same pain and anger that you may be feeling.

- When you make a focused effort to remove the negative from your life, you create positive thinking and a positive environment.

- When you really focus on being true to yourself, honestly asking and telling who you are, and embracing your passion for your work, for your life, confidence is yours for keeps.

- When you understand that always doing things they way you have always done them stifles you, you value being different and breaking a few of the old rules . . . the sacred cows. The buzz goes out that you are either innovative, a risk taker, a change master, or a troublemaker. How you proceed will be your Mecca or Waterloo.

The *10 Steps of Building Confidence* are on a continuing circle; each one linked one to the other. By circulating, you will circulate each step, hopefully on a daily basis.

Talk to Me

Many of the men and women surveyed said that it was important to talk to someone—to get feedback, a reality check as to what was really going on. Getting feedback and interacting with others is critical for development. It doesn't matter if you are two years old or seventy years old.

Get help, any kind of help. If you are unemployed, get counseling help; there are groups that will assist you when moneys are minimal. If you are having problems with your bills, get credit counseling. Even psychiatric foundations in cities offer free counseling for those who can't pay if money is short.

Whatever kind of help, you can get, get it and don't be afraid of it. If there is a self-help group for people who are out of work or for people who are down on their luck, seek it out and go as often as you can. If you can find something like that every day to go to, it actually becomes a positive thing to look forward to.

One of the side issues that occur in confidence crushing scenarios is that of "if only," or the Scarlett O'Hare approach, "Tomorrow's another day." Don't get stuck on them. When you get reality checks and feedback, you are able to move on and not be stuck in the "tomorrows" and "if onlys" of your life. Consider doing jobs, chores, and things in a five-minute timeframe versus a block of the entire afternoon. Literally, one step at a time.

If you have one leg in tomorrow and one in yesterday, you're sabotaging today. If you have one leg in tomorrow and one in yesterday, you are paralyzed. Trusted others can give you appropriate feedback, encourage you to move on and make today the real thing versus fantasy.

Is Your Net Working?

As you read through this step, you may feel that it sounds like networking. In some ways, it is. Networking has been typically viewed as a means of getting something—contacts, visibility, and promotion. Networking is much more and needs to be looked at with new glasses. It should involve team play—passing information around, spreading the unwritten rules of the business world, giving praise to others, and being there when they are down. Or out.

Ideally, feedback should be positive. Ideally. In reality, some feedback may be negative. If anything, it needs to be "appropriate." Undeserved criticism or feedback rarely helps anyone.

Networking and feedback go hand in hand. Any feedback must be honest and constructive. If you have been asked for input by a trusted friend or colleague, what you may have to say may not be 100 percent terrific. Or you may be the recipient of not 100 percent positive feedback. Before you open your mouth, or your ears, ask yourself, is it honest? Is it constructive? Will it help unravel the situation?

Susan RoAne is known by many as the mingling maven. RoAne is the expert on networking. She's written several books, all bestsellers. Her latest is *How to Work a Room*, which is a terrific bible for getting out on your feet again. She feels it's essential to keep up with your networking colleagues. Not just a network where you hand out business cards. Rather, a network that knows about the challenges and opportunities within your own specific arena. RoAne says,

Networking to me has been the single most valuable tool in my growth as a professional, an activist, and a communicator. I see it as an action item for every man and woman. Many think of networking as everyone telling what they do and then passing out business cards. Networking is way beyond that.

Networking is an action you can indulge in. It's certainly not the "be all" and "end all," but it's right up there on top. I believe in networking for the purpose of helping others. I don't presume that by networking I will get something back. If that happens, it's terrific, it's a bonus. You always have chits out there that can be collected, but you don't engage in it for the purpose of collecting a chit. It's a fine line and needs to be recognized as such. It's a skill that I've had and have honed.

Savvy networking is beyond telling people who I am, what I do, and passing my business card out.

Creating Support

Having a support group forces you to come out. Speaker and trainer Leslie Charles definitely feels that the support group is one of the key things that kept her going when she was that welfare mother—the woman from the west side of Lansing, Michigan, who was waiting for Mr. Right to come along and marry her kids and her.

Sometimes my support group was just one person, sometimes two. There has always been someone there for me to talk to, so I don't have to bottle things up and I can get the feedback I need. I have a high encouragement level and a high level of trust. Most of the time I get rewarded for that. I have been strong and that is one of the things that has helped me through the bumpy periods of my life. I believe that all of us need psychological answers—sometimes family, sometimes with friends, sometimes professional colleagues, and sometimes professionals whose time I pay for.

Not all professional counselors are in synch with you. Years ago, my family sought a counselor for some guidance during our kids' rebellious teen years. We saw someone who I thought was very good. After a few sessions, we had a family powwow meeting. All of us agreed he wasn't the right fit. Maybe for someone else, but not for us. We went shopping for a new therapist. Don't just turn over your life to anyone and assume that he or she will fix it. The person who fixes it is you. Only you.

Host/producer Yue-Sal Kan adds her word of warning. She feels that psychiatrists are not the cure-all, and, in fact, can be destructive if you have the wrong fit. She is a believer in the support system, and getting appropriate feedback:

I personally do not go to a psychiatrist. Psychiatrists allow you the luxury of repeating your misery over and over again. They encourage you to "talk it out." I have found that when I am unhappy about something, and I talk about it repeatedly, I reinforce my negative feelings over and over again. The result is that I am even unhappier! To me, repeating negative feelings is a form of negative visualization that can lead to further erosion of confidence and ego.

What I do instead is that I first acknowledge what's happened, allow myself a good cry, then, always immediately, I discipline myself to push this unhappy episode out of my thoughts and my mind. I force myself to other diversions, totally submerging myself in things that have nothing to do with the unhappiness. It may sound hard, but I have done it many times. I am always amazed at how I can sometimes totally obliterate something very unhappy from my head. It is *my* way of protecting myself.

You may have friends who are brilliant and offer lots of help, but sometimes when you are feeling so uncomfortable about who you are or what you have just experienced that it makes sense to talk to somebody that will allow you to be totally honest and not judgmental.

Although your best friends shouldn't make judgments about you, there may be something in your relationship that might hold them back from saying what you really need to hear.

Not bottling things up and getting feedback, appropriate feedback, is a critical element in getting, growing, and keeping confidence. Not everyone agreed on whom the feedback should come from, but they did agree that it was important to get it. Sometimes that feedback will come from a woman, a parent, a family member, a therapist, your mate, your children, a colleague at work—male or female, someone who knows you as you.

A word of caution: whoever it is that you seek feedback from, to talk to, to share your fears, your pain, your hurt, your joys, it should be someone who respects you. Not only respects you as a person, but respects your values. Don't just talk to anybody, at any time. *Discriminate.* Talk with someone who will give you feedback. It may be a long-term relationship, a friend, a crony, a colleague, partner, or family member.

It should definitely not be someone that you have just met and are only acquainted with on a casual basis. This is one of the fatal errors that too many make. How many times have you met someone and within minutes, she reveals her whole life story to you? And, how many times have you met someone and within minutes, you have shared yours? Life stories, problems, concerns, hopes and dreams are not just for anyone's ears. Choose your feedback partners wisely. They should be caring and supportive of you as a person and non-judgmental. A tall request that few can fill.

Keeper #18
Maintaining and keeping your visibility is a key factor in rebuilding confidence. Don't disappear when the chips are down. Ever.

Staying in circulation is a must in building confidence. But where you get it from will either add to your foundation or will further tumble your tower of confidence.

Chapter Eleven

Step #10

Show Courage . . . Forget-it-Not

We want to build something the world hasn't seen.
Jeff Bezos, CEO
Amazon.com

When we asked our respondents if they were able to say "no" when someone told them that they had to do something that was a wrong fit for them, men showed more courage in speaking out with 61% versus 45% for women saying that they *often* said no to what they deemed the wrong fit. *Always* respondents were 10% women and 9% men. The men and women were close in the *rarely* category with 7% of the men saying so and 6% of the women stating that no just wasn't in their vocabulary and 39% of the women and 23% of the men said that *sometimes* they said no, but mostly they said yes.

We also asked if they ever got caught saying yes, when their druthers was to say no, which takes courage at times. Our respondents were quite close. In the *always* category, none of the men said they did, with 1% of the women saying so. *Often* respondents were 16% each for men and women; *sometimes* at 48% for women and 42% for men; and finally, 35% of the women and 42% of the men saying that they *rarely* got looped into committing to something when they didn't want to.

The New New Thing

For two decades, I lived in Silicon Valley. I moved there in 1972, joining EF Hutton as a stockbroker, later creating my own company and selling it in 1986. Since then, I have dedicated my "work" energies to writing and speaking.

As one of the "new kids" on the block in 1972, I was oblivious to what Silicon Valley was all about, literally clueless. But I learned and what I discovered in the process was the depth and range of courage of the men and women of the Valley. Companies were created during that time that would revolutionize how we lived and worked. Companies that were birthed from the mother ship eventually gobbled it up and created new offspring. No single book exemplifies the Valley as well as Michael Lewis' *The New New Thing* which profiles Jim Clark and the billion dollar empires he's created . . . over and over.

Clark had the courage to say enough was enough after the "take over" of Silicon Graphics (now known as SGI) by the outsiders, micro-managers who were extraordinarily naïve—or some say downright stupid—about how to run the company and interact with its people.

When Clark finally said adiós to Silicon Graphics in 1994, his next venture was Netscape. This time, Clark rewrote the rules—from when the company would go public to how the "core" employees would get compensated with stock to what equity positions the venture capitalists would be allowed and at what price they bought in.

For the first time, the engineers—the men and women who created the codes and programs that drove a company—hit the jackpot. When Netscape went public, it's stock quadrupled the first day. Those who did the real work, not just the money people, came out on top. Netscape made them multi-millionaires.

Jim Clark was so stung by his treatment at SGI, that he basically said, "Never again." Granted, Clark is different. He's also brilliant. He doesn't live in the past, barely the present. What he does is project the future as only an engineer who intimately understands the breadth and use of technology can. The day that Netscape traded stock, SGI became a sick company—no longer viewed as a vision of the future. Jim Clark was the vision and wherever Clark went, others wanted to follow.

Empire Builders

No one person on the Internet exemplifies empire building as Amazon.com's CEO, Jeff Bezos. In just a few short years, his vision has changed they way millions of people shop. Amazon.com is the superstore of superstores. And it, like many of the corporate stars of today, started in a garage in Seattle in 1994.

One of my favorite sayings is, "Books fall open and

you fall in." So it is with Amazon. Once you get online, once you got to the site, once you make your first purchase, once you sign up for "one-click," you get the bug. You fall in. Bezos made the Internet safe for shopping, few are concerned that their stored credit card numbers will be violated. Millions spend billions on the site. During the Holiday season of 2000, Amazon shipped over 33 million items around the world! Bezos says,

> We want to build something the world hasn't seen. The Internet is a big, huge hurricane. The only constant in that storm is the customer.

It takes courage to even contemplate building something the world hasn't seen. Bezos reminds me of Star Trek—boldly going where no one has gone before. His goal was to create the most customer-oriented store anywhere—be it bricks and mortar, out of the home, or on the Web. Bezos dismissed the common belief that Web users were merely surfing and checking out site after site. He believed that if you treated your customers exceptionally well; if you learned who they were and what they wanted and offered it to them; and you did it all exceeding fast, they were yours. And right he was.

Taking Care of Yourself

Being courageous also means that you have to take the time to take care of yourself. CEO Jean Kelley almost lost her business due to her drinking years ago.

> My business was brand new and I thought I was going to lose it if I didn't quit drinking; it's all I ever

had. I never had any kids; I never had anything that was mine except the business I stayed up nights with when it was sick, even diapering it. I brought it through adolescence. It's part of me. I finally realized that if I didn't quit drinking that I was going to damage or kill this child of mine. Or me.

My drinking was like driving on an empty street and hitting a patch of ice. Like losing your brakes and sailing along, knowing you are going to hit something if you don't stop. In your sober moments, you wonder if you can't stop in time, what will you hit? You are totally out of control.

I felt that I was in that type of motion with my drinking. I was struggling with all my might and pretty soon I would disappear into the abyss of alcohol. I knew it. At last, I didn't have any problem admitting that I was an alcoholic. I had known since I was nineteen years old and I thought, 'You've worked your whole life to build this business. You are twenty-six years old. What do you want to do? Ruin it?'

So I called up a few of my friends who were also alcoholics. They had recently quit drinking. I asked if they would take me to an AA meeting. And the night before I went, I confessed that I was quite drunk. A friend of mine said, 'Can you just not drink for today? Can you just not drink one day?' And I told her I could do it. But on that day, I didn't know how challenging it would be. I had a date with a man who was a real drinker. I resisted and got through it. I never drank again.

Encouraged All the Way

Host-Producer Yue-Sai Kan believes that courage and risk taking go hand-in-hand—from yourself and those who support you. In her case, her family was willing to risk plenty to create the window of opportunity for her.

First of all, they nurtured me to the point that they felt that they wanted me to develop. They then allowed me to do. I wanted to come to America to school, they supported me. I wanted to learn ballet; they would get me the best ballet teacher and would encourage me. If I wanted to learn French, they would find me the best French teacher. When I wanted to play the piano, they found me the best piano teacher.

Sure enough, I became a very talented pianist when I was a child. I excelled at ballet and French. All my life I've had the encouragement from my teachers and my parents. They instilled in me that not only did I have the responsibility of being the firstborn; I also have the talent to learn and the ability to achieve whatever I want to do.

Initially, when I wanted to come to America, my parents were not for the idea, but I wanted it and they supported it. Eventually, they followed me and they now also live in New York. When I decided to enter the television arena, they were not too encouraging, but they did not discourage me.

When I had the opportunity to come to America, I entered a country where dreams can be made. That is, providing you are willing to work hard and do it in an intelligent manner. In America, you can excel.

Yue-Sai Kan believes there is a special spirit still in America. For her, America will always be a place for the talented, the hard working, and for anyone who is willing to take risks. All it takes is courage.

Keeper #19
When you allow yourself to be open, examining and assessing whatever the issue is and maintaining your integrity, vistas expand. Opportunities arrive. It's rather like a leap of faith.

Standing Tall

Few of us will have to face the cold metal of a gun barrel to find out what our level of courage is. Management consultant and author Nicole Shapiro did. Her memories of her upbringing begin at the age of one and a half. The time, World War II. The place, Budapest. She can remember watching her mother from her highchair when three men with tall, shining black boots and uniforms came into the room. Each had a whip and a gun. They were Nazis.

One of them grabbed my mother's arms and threatened to kill her and the baby (me) if she wouldn't tell them where the Jews were. Though I was only one and a half years of age, I can still remember the cold metal of the gun barrel on my head. My mother stood up, all five feet tall of her, and had direct eye contact with the tallest of the soldiers. To this day, I swear that as she rose, she became even taller than the men. My mother responded that she didn't know where the Jews were, that they could shoot her daughter and herself, but she didn't know where any were.

The atmosphere in the little room was both dead and electric. At the same time, what I have learned to be 'confidence' permeated the air. My mother had made a commitment to do what she had to do. To protect the other Jews, friends of hers in the homes next door. I saw my mother's confidence transfuse her with strength. That strength has been carried with me since I was that toddler. The powers from my mother and the upbringing that I experienced have been and still are major factors in my life today.

Today, companies in the Fortune 500 seek out Nicole Schapiro's management expertise. Her books, *The Dance of Negotiation—How to Level the Playing Field* and *Negotiating for Your Life,* are musts for anyone trying to improve his or her life. The principles her mother demonstrated and taught her as a child were carried over during the Hungarian Revolution where she found herself in a firing line. She has been able to integrate the subtle messages her mother demonstrated to her over fifty-five years ago with her consulting and speaking business that stresses both negotiation and team building. All done with risk taking and displaying courage as key factors.

Quack, Quack

When Don and Lucy Hillestad founded the Hillestad Corporation, a company that focused on health and nutrition, they received a lot of flack from people in the community. To overcome the preconceived ideas and prejudices of many took courage. They said,

> There are many times that we had to pick ourselves up by the bootstraps and say, 'What you are doing is right and what's happening to you is right, but what's happened is wrong. Keep doing what your heart and what your passion is about.'

Both of the Hillestads liken themselves to bulldogs. They hang on to the piece of rope and will not let go. We have to believe in ourselves and believe in the sort of things that we are involved in. Lucy continues,

> We learned a long time ago that it does not have to be normal for our children to catch dozens of colds and to have tooth decay and have broken bones. You can raise a family without having broken bones, tooth decay, and every disease that everyone else in the neighborhood has.
>
> When we started talking about our philosophy of health care and forming our business around that premise, people would attack us. In fact, they would laugh at us and make fun of us. When they saw us coming down the street, they would say, 'You're a

quack.' When they would see us walk in, I would hear, 'Quack, quack.'

If anything ever happened negatively in the nutrition industry, they would quote it in the paper. People would run over to us and point it out to show how wrong we were and that we thinking in the wrong direction. But, we kept on track.

Both of us come from farming. My dad always wanted to get first prize at the county fair when he took his pigs, his chickens, and his cows there. And how did he get the first prize? He fed them well. He gave them everything possible to make their coats shiny, to make them have strong hindquarters. He knew exactly what to do.

I asked myself, 'Why can't I do the same thing for my kids? Wouldn't I want my kids to get the blue ribbon at the fair?' Absolutely. How would I get my blue ribbon? By having healthy children. The solution was simple. It was right in our pocketbook. I wasn't going to have all the doctor bills, the dentist bills, the hospital bills, and the like that everyone else did. It made sense.

We didn't have much money in the family, there were ten kids. But my Dad made sure we sat down at the table three times a day to eat. It also made sense to him that he gives supplements to support the health of the cows, the chickens, and the pigs so that they had good reproduction. He always got good yields on his crops because he fed the ground with supplements and nutrients. He knew in the end that it made a difference in his pocketbook. When I thought about my own family, I really saw no difference.

The Hillestads have been nutrition business for over 45 years. There is no question that it has been financially good for them. There were bumpy times, but they hung in because they believed in what they were doing. They have been invited to the White House to participate in nutritional conferences and are well known in their field.

They believe that any little success helps your confidence to grow. By keeping your eye on the ball or on your goals, you can start putting little marks down to review what those goals are. Persevering and believing in self have been their mainstays for everything they do—self, relationships, family, and for their business.

Bridging the Globe

Where Jeff Bezos brought shopping to the masses, Steve Case is responsible for bringing the Internet to the masses. His America Online changed the way the average person communicates. From kids to seniors, people are just a phone line and finger taps away. As the world becomes wireless, the need for the traditional phone live vanishes. Where Amazon still reported red ink at the end of 2000, AOL has been in the black, reporting positive earnings for several years.

Steve Case has proven himself one of the savviest entrepreneur's today. With an announcement that stunned the corporate world in 2000, AOL set out to merge with Time Warner—a stable commodity in the corporate marketplace. The end result is that it created the world's largest media business when approved in 2001.

Just where did this guy come from? How did he put it together? How come CNN's Ted Turner (who sold to

Time Warner and sits on the its Board) not think of it? Turner later reported that it was one of the most exciting deals he had even seen put together.

In looking back, the project that Jim Clark envisioned at SGI, involved several of the concepts of what Case sees for AOL-Time Warner. Instead of doing all the communicating and entertaining via the television set as SGI proposed, AOL's window was the PC. Case says,

> Instead of viewing the PC as a productivity machine, we've turned it into a communication device. It's about building a sense of community and engaging people.

Plenty of corporate people grumble about the slowness they've experience using AOL. Most corporations use their own servers, not needing all the features that AOL offers to its customers. The fact that corporate America doesn't use it doesn't matter—the masses use it, which is what it was designed for. Over 20 million subscribers fork over roughly $20 a month to talk, shop, get information and be entertained around the world.

Courageous people are successful. When you are considered successful, to have made it—more demands (and people) make their path to your door. Most will be quite reasonable and flattering. The timing, though, is sometimes out of synch with your ability to take on, or want to take on, more duties and responsibilities. It takes courage to tell others "no." Steve Case, Jeff Bezos, Nicole Schapiro, the Hillestads, Jean Kelly, Yue-Sai Kan and Jim Clark all had to tell others no to stay on track to create their vision and dream.

> *Keeper #20*
> *Courage is the catalyst of change.*
> *Without it, creativity is stifled.*
> *Growth is stunted.*
> *Great ideas and concepts die.*

As Dorothy's goal to get home was diverted by the wants, wishes, and demands of the inhabitants of Oz, she allowed herself to stay focused: "I want to go home." She prioritized her need to leave Oz, and as each new demand was placed on her, she was able finally to make it conditional on her returning to Kansas. Dorothy could have been the Wizardess of Oz if she had wanted the title. Her success in fending off Oz's enemies could have gotten in her way of returning home if she let it. She didn't.

Harry Potter finds himself tied up in ropes at the end of *The Sorcerer's Stone*. The evil Quirrell has linked his own soul with the more evil Lord Voldemort, who killed Harry's parents when he was a baby. Granted, he's destined to be a great wizard, but he's only a small boy when he meets up with Quirrell. Cunningly, and certainly with courage, Harry attempts to distract Quirrell and Voldemort so that he can figure out a way to find and save the magic Stone. The duo tries to trick Harry into revealing how to get the Stone out. The race/fight is on. But, because of who and what Harry is, it ends up in his pocket. He didn't give up and ultimately succeeded in outwitting his adversaries.

Nor should you.

Chapter Twelve

Cosmic Gooses Are Your Golden Eggs

I see things as always evolving, a work in progress. I need to feel that I am a good craftsperson and that I can do my work well. Finally, I feel my life is being shaped by a higher power; that understanding and knowledge make me feel confident, but whatever happens is not mistake.

Olympia Dukakis,
Actress

In interviewing and writing *The Confidence Factor*, thousands of men and women have shared their thoughts; some have exposed their deep pain felt in crises, while others have been quite philosophical about theirs.

Through these thousands of voices, three basics surface—to build confidence you need knowledge—*experience, success,* and *control.* This does not mean that you will not have failures—those *cosmic gooses*. If you allow them, failures lead to success—yours.

Remember your first times when you attempting to drive a car? Gaining knowledge and experience is similar. Your hands gripped the steering wheel, and then one day you realized you could actually drive with one hand and wave the other at a friend. You felt a little smarter, a little more comfortable; your confidence got a boost. You were a legit driver!

Finally, in order to have confidence, control is needed. Control in the form of "hands-on" as you are actively involved in a project and complete many of the steps. The second part of that is once you have been successful, you need to know what the steps were in leading to your success.

Keeper #21
Don't do well what you have no business doing. So stay focused; be passionate and keep learning.

The getting, keeping, and growing of confidence is similar to a continuum of births—births and rebirths that came through dreams and visions, through the school of hard knocks, through failure, through hope, through fear, through risk, through stretching, through success, through life. None of it will be handed to you without strings. Some of the strings will be in a pay-forward approach—reach out and pass on what you have received. Others will land you on your rear, you have to regroup.

You are the hero or heroine of your life—a journey that you will have to reshape and redirect through a series of mazes that everyday living presents. It can be either an adventure or the nightmare of a dungeon. More likely, it will have some of each. If you learn to do what you fear, your fear will not control you.

When you fall into the dungeons that failure, crises, and the wrong upbringing can bring, it is easy to be slain. You may be out for the count for a while, even near what you think is death. With the *10 Steps of Building Confidence* as a guide, you will be able to climb out of the dungeon, get back into the adventure and reinvent yourself. Your journey into confidence will be like a stage—at times all the lights will be up, at times there will be loud music/noises, at others dim lights, subtle touches. You don't get the opportunity to rehearse your life as an actor does on a stage. Rather, you jump right in and live the part with all its glory and sorrow, unbeknownst to you which acts will create turbulence, which ones bliss.

If you presently have storms brewing at work or at home; if nothing appears to be what you think it is or should be, think about what advertising would like us all to believe is a woman's best friend—the diamond. You. Only think of a diamond in its roughest form—it's a dull, whitish, unattractive stone. It appears to have zero value. Yet, underneath, enormous potential. If cut and polished by a master cutter, its dull luster turns to brilliance. Its value skyrockets. If, on the other hand, it is cut improperly and not polished, the value could be nothing at all.

You have that possibility of brilliance, of being able to shine like the most brilliant diamond. Your brilliance comes from within. Telling yourself that you have all the raw material that anyone will ever need to build confidence is your beginning. Don't give it away. Now is the time for you to symbolically click the heels of your silver shoes, as Dorothy did, or surround yourself with the invisible cloak as Harry Potter did and claim, own, and expand the confidence that you possess.

All of us need some form of success, whether it's a promotion, praise on the job, or getting credit. The road to your success can be invisibly cloaked—some with detours, some with awesome potholes, some with a cosmic goose or two. Those obstacles become confidence building blocks.
  Your Golden Eggs.

Acknowledgements

Books are like great soups and stews. Initially, the idea sounds good, but doesn't become great until all the ingredients are added and allowed to simmer. In the case of *The Confidence Factor*, the ingredients became the people I met along the way.

Ronnie Moore and WESType once again created magic inside the covers. Mikell Yamada quickly grasped my vision for the cover. I thank them both.

As always, Marilyn Ross was generous with answers and solutions to just about any question I had. Joe Sabah was, and is, every author's enthusiastic cheerleader. Thank you both.

Ron Rice was incredible and creative in designing the Internet component for the survey used. He is the best in Web Mastering.

Shari Peterson, John Maling and Jerusha Stewart sharpened pencils and eyes—always responding to my query—does this make sense and does it flow?

The Confidence Factor—Cosmic Gooses Lay Golden Eggs contains thousands of voices of women and men today. I thank them for their time and sharing.

About the Author
Judith Briles, PhD, MBA

Dr. Judith Briles is CEO of The Briles Group, Inc a Colorado based research, training and consulting firm. She is internationally acclaimed as a keynote speaker and recognized as an expert in solutions to workplace issues.

She is an award winning author of over 20 books including *Woman to Woman 2000, Changing Conflict to Collaboration, 10 Smart Money Moves for Women, Smart Money Moves for Kids, The Dollars and Sense of Divorce, GenderTraps,* and *Stop Stabbing Yourself in the Back.*

Dr. Briles has been featured on over 1000 radio and television programs nationwide and writes columns for the *Denver Business Journal, Colorado Woman News, MsMoney.com and iSpiritus.com.* Her work has been featured in The Wall Street Journal, Time, People, USA Today and the New York Times. She's a frequent guest on MSNBC, CNNfn and CNN.

For information about Judith Briles' availability for speeches and subscribing to her newsletter, contact her at:

Judith@Briles.com or DrJBriles@aol.com
www.Briles.com

303-627-9179 ~ 303-627-9184 Fax
The Briles Group, Inc.
14160 E. Bellewood Dr.
Aurora, CO 80015

Also by
Dr. Judith Briles

Changing Conflict to Collaboration
Stop Stabbing Yourself in the Back
Woman to Woman 2000
The Briles Report on Women in Healthcare
10 Smart Money Moves for Women
Smart Money Moves for Kids
The Dollars and Sense of Divorce
GenderTraps
Confidence—How Self Esteem Can Change Your Life
When God Says NO
Money Sense
The Money $ense Guidebook
Raising Money-Wise Kids
Woman to Woman
Judith Briles' Money Book
Faith & $avvy Too!
Money Phases
The Woman's Guide to Financial Savvy
The Workplace
Self-Confidence and Peak Performance
Divorce the Financial Guide for Women

Free articles and information on Judith's books
are available on her web site at www.Briles.com.